THIS COLORING BOOK BELONGS TO:

____

AND IS MEANT TO INSPIRE YOU TO TRAVEL THE WORLD!

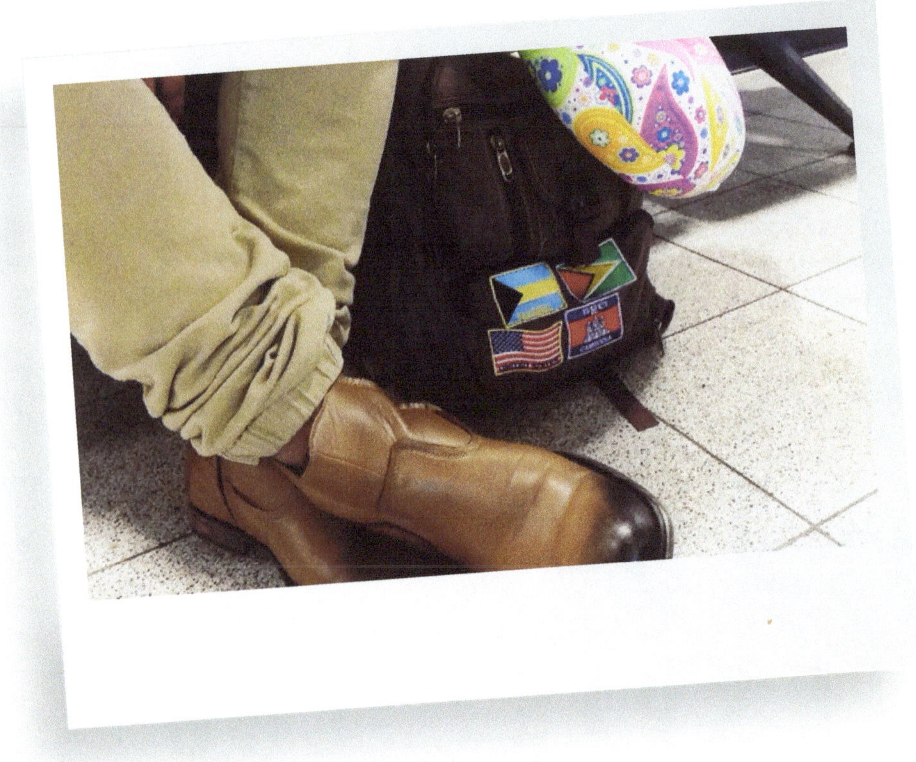

AIRPORT

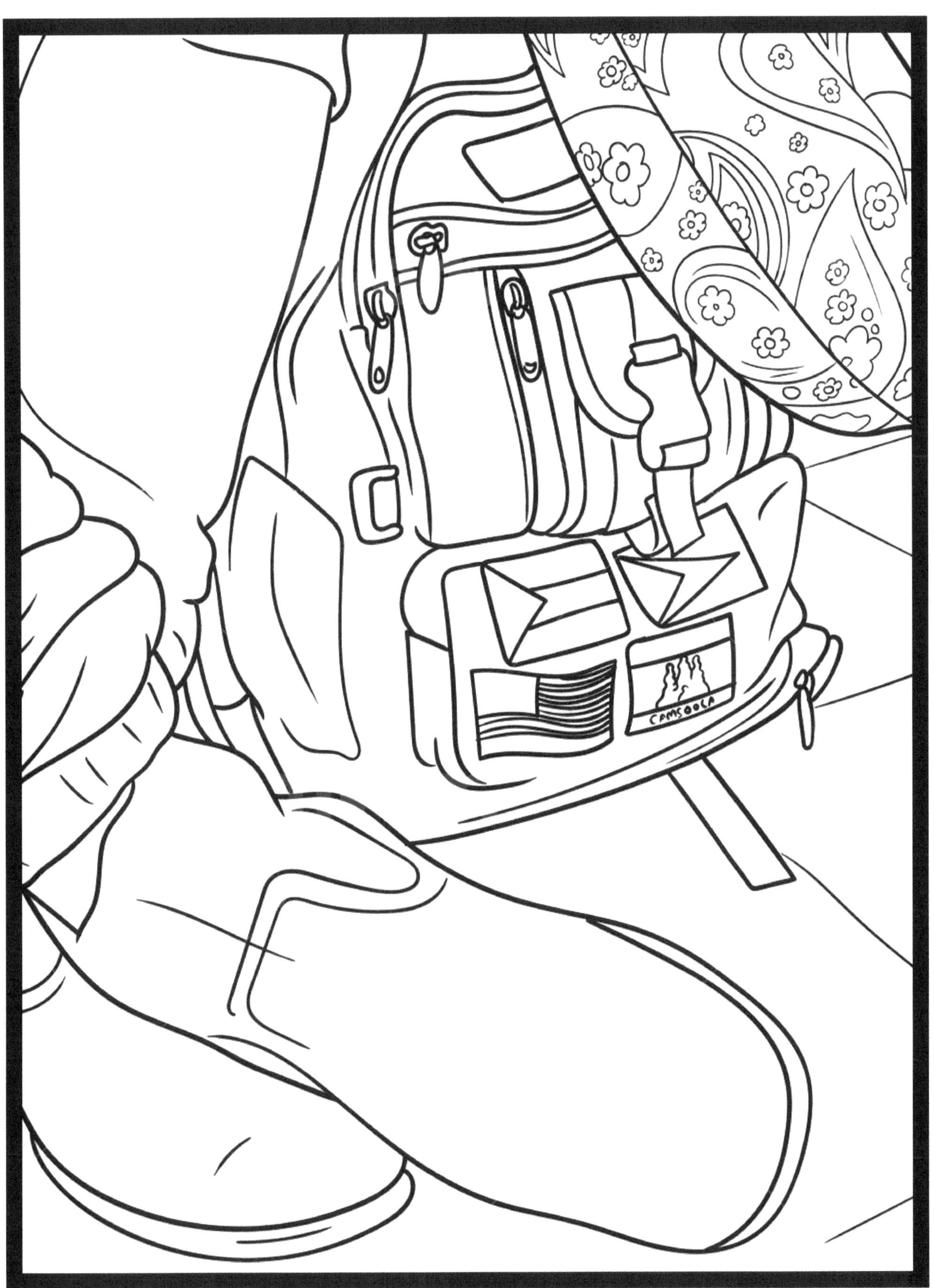

CAMSOOCA

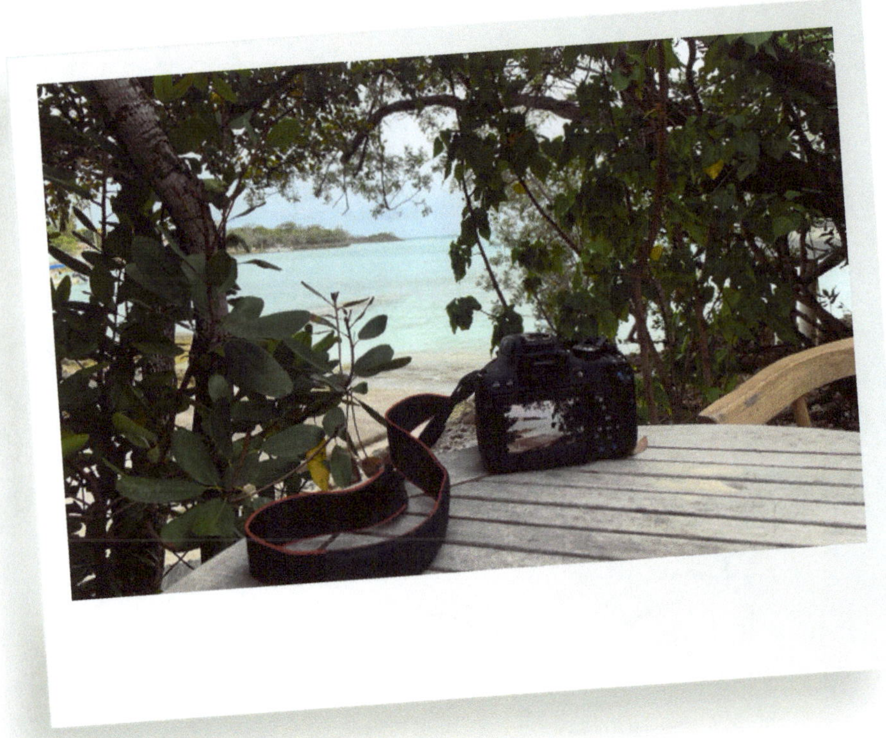

CAMERA

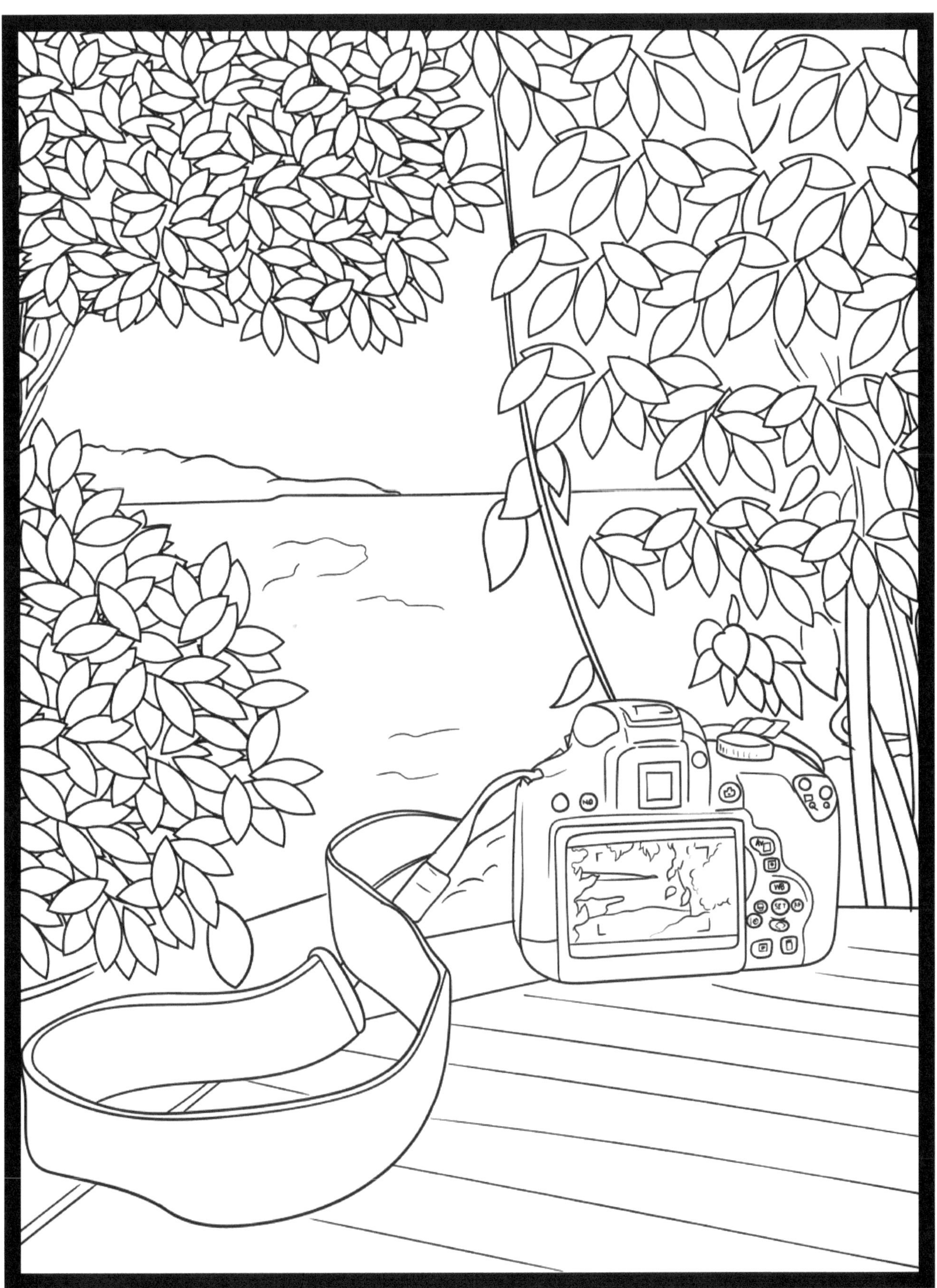

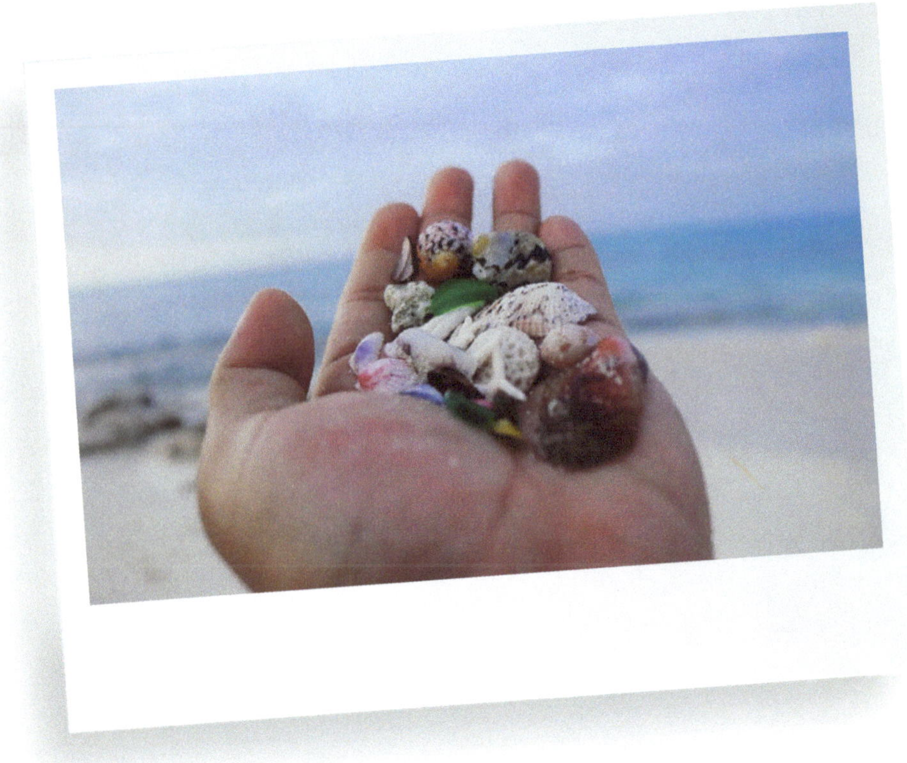

NASSAU, BAHAMAS

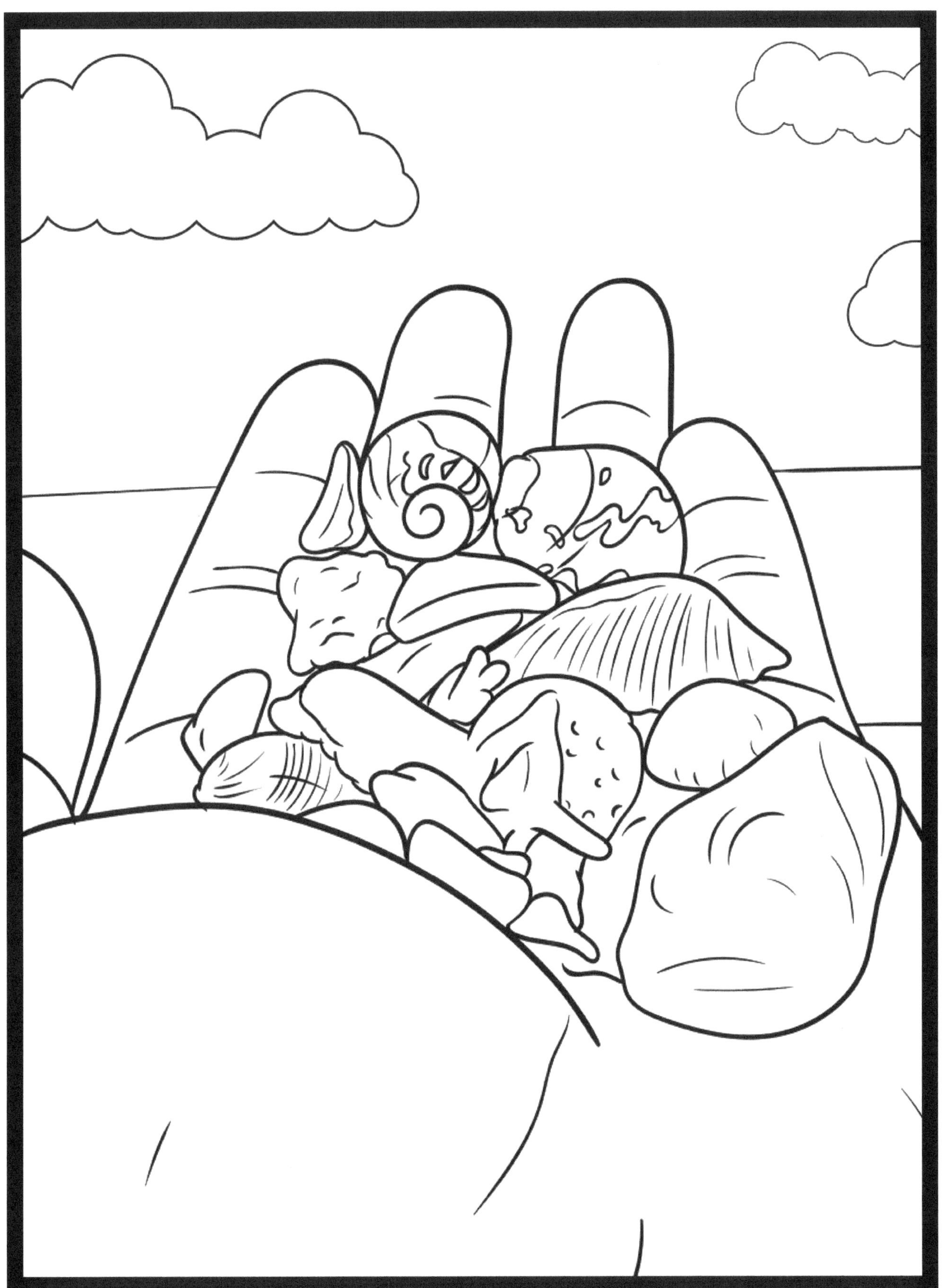

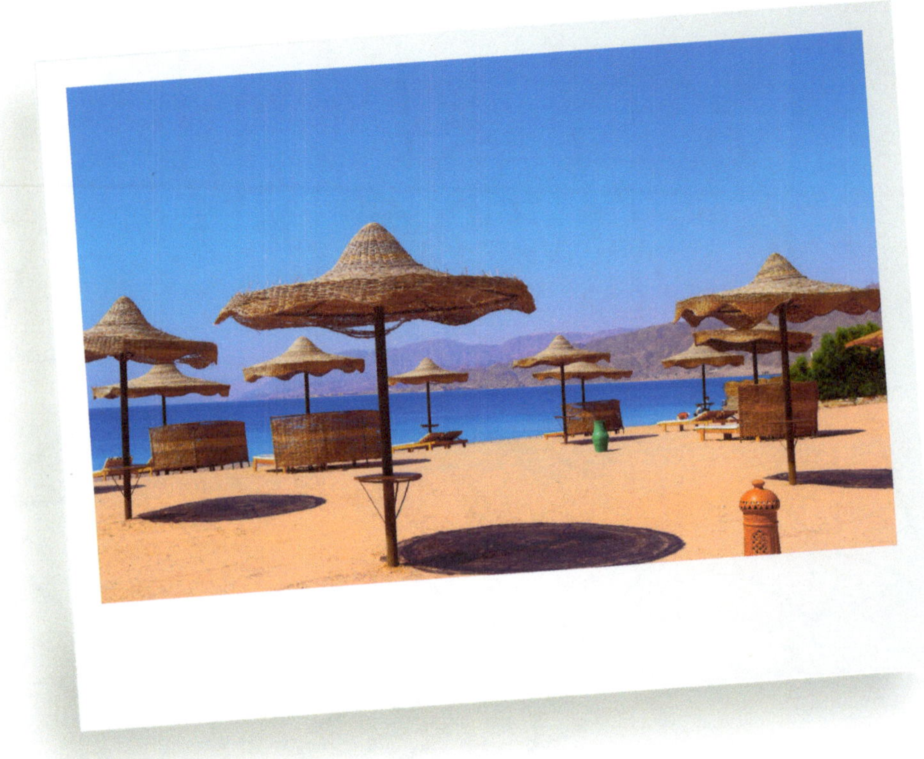

TABA, EGYPT

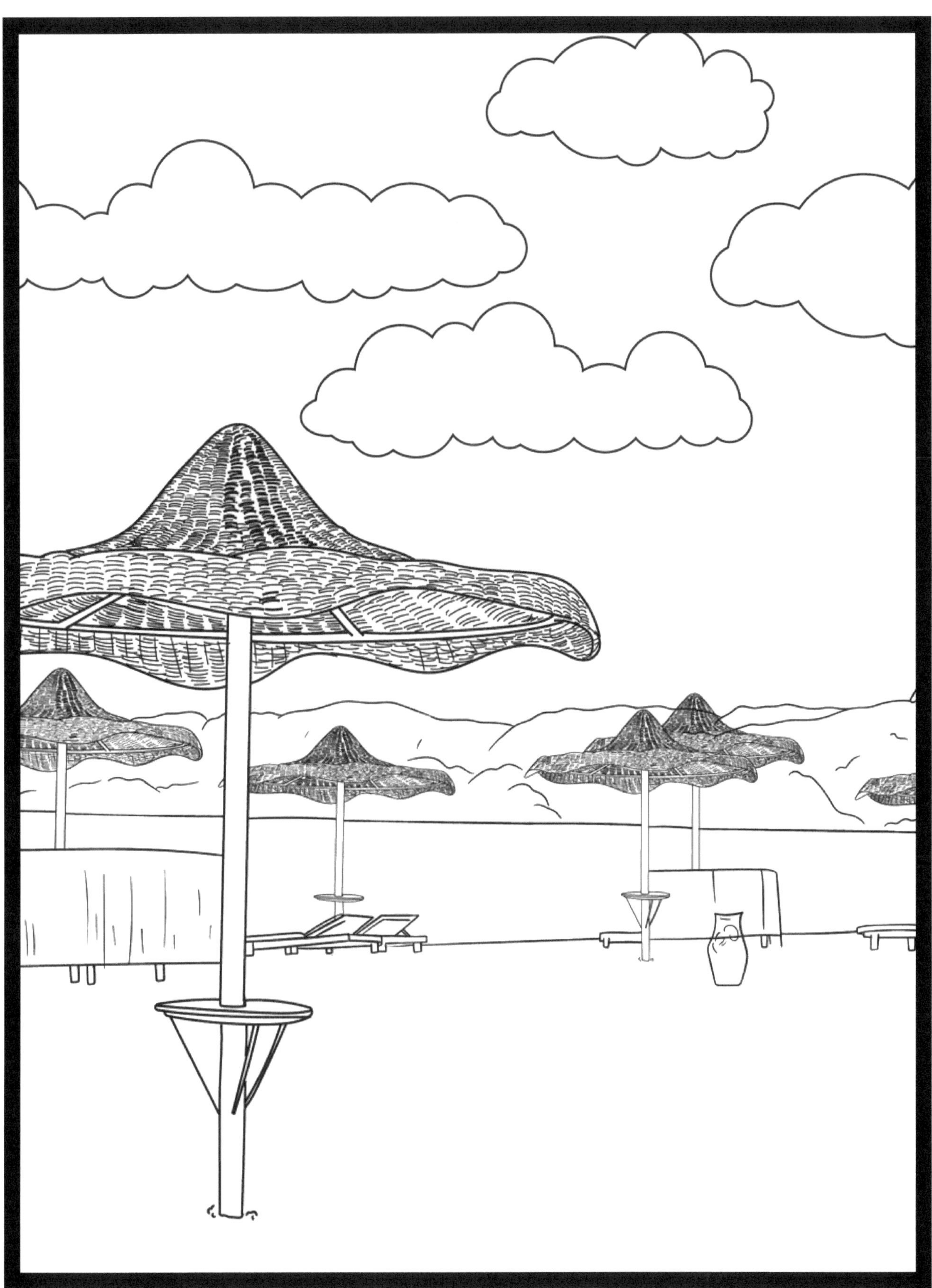

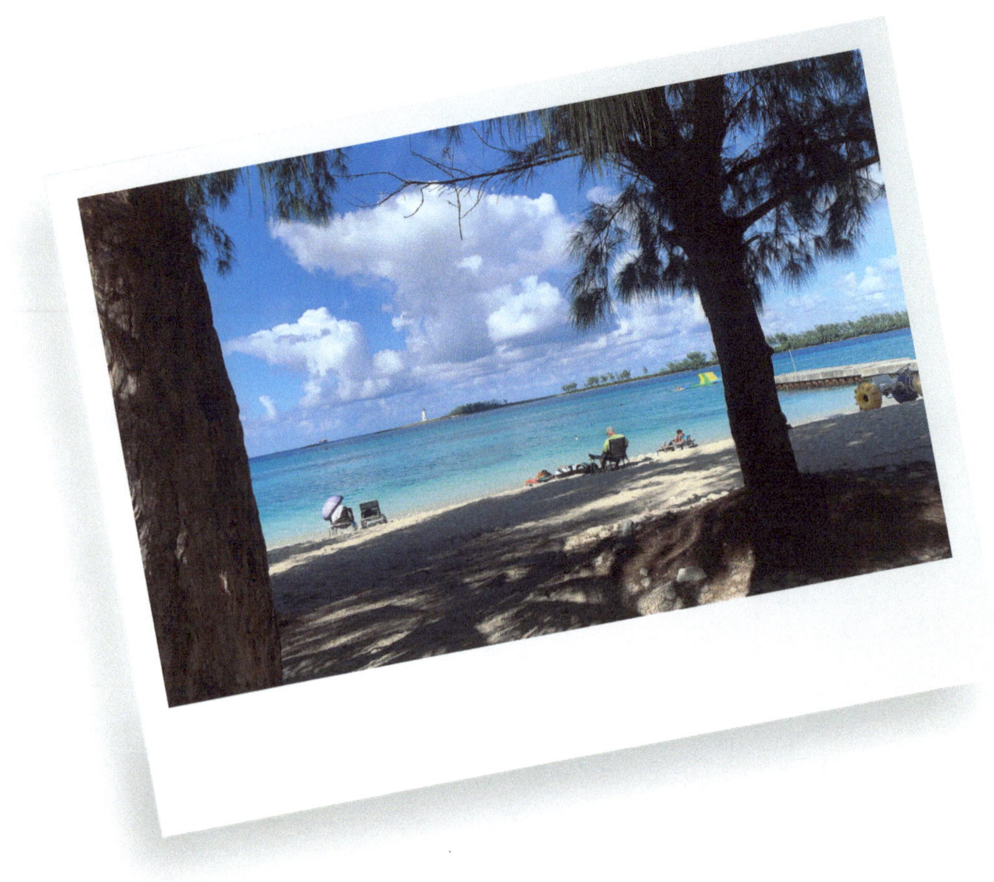

NASSAU, BAHAMAS

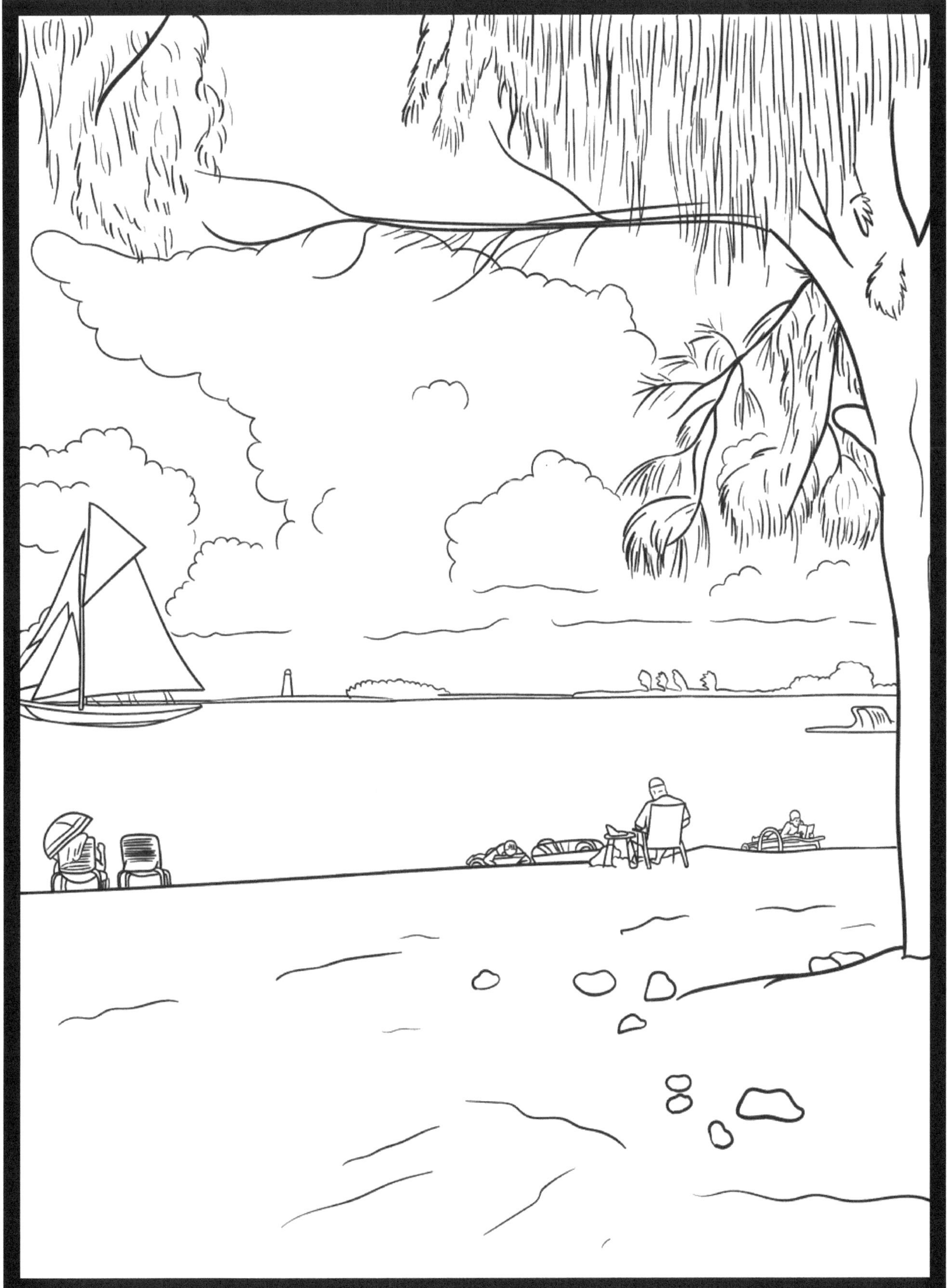

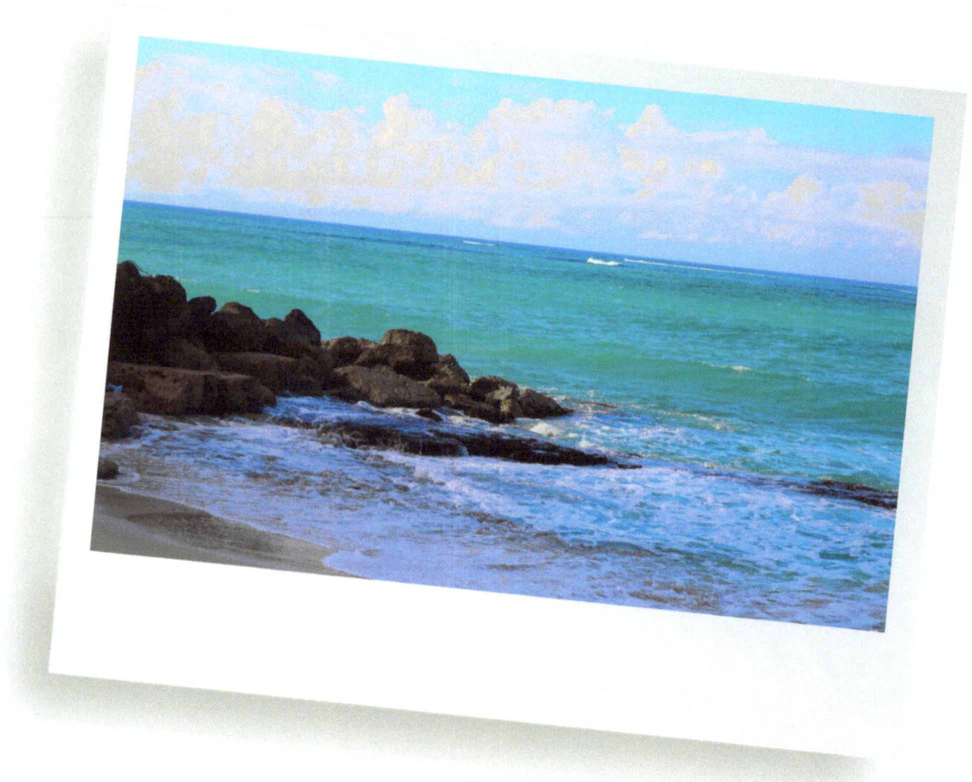

NASSAU, BAHAMAS

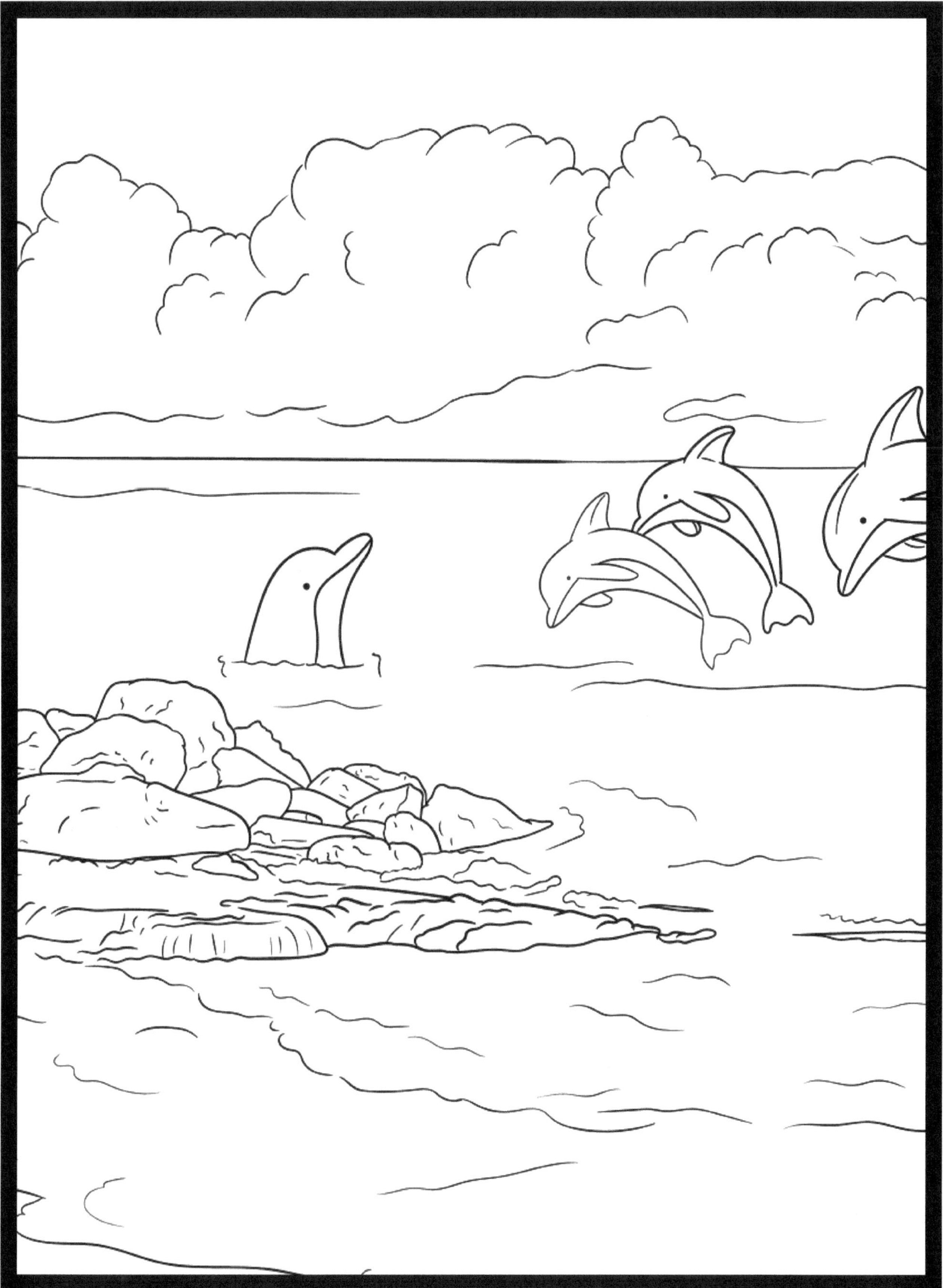

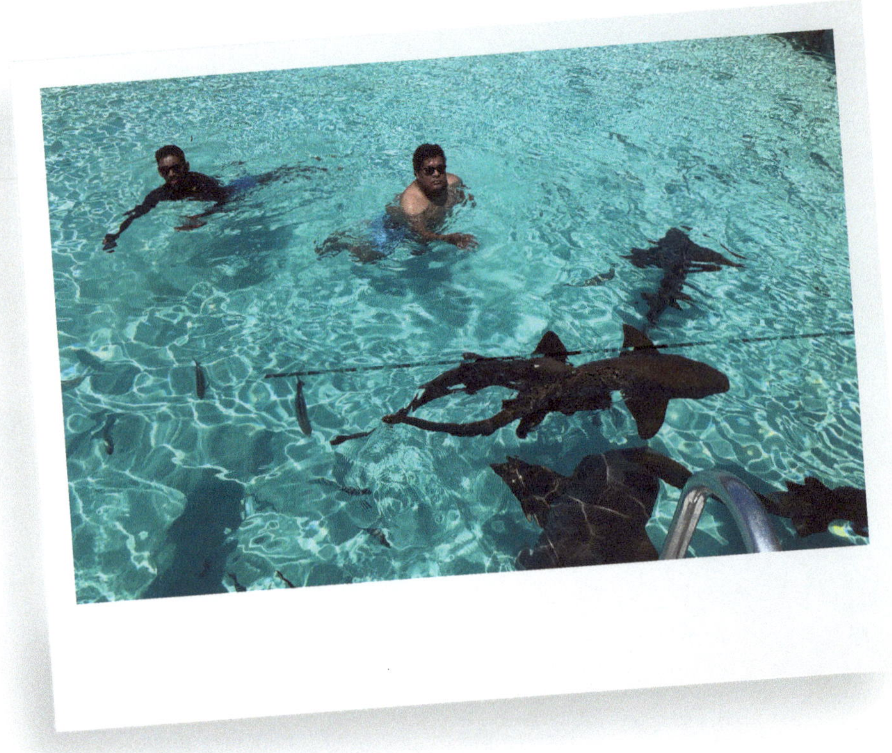

EXUMA, BAHAMAS

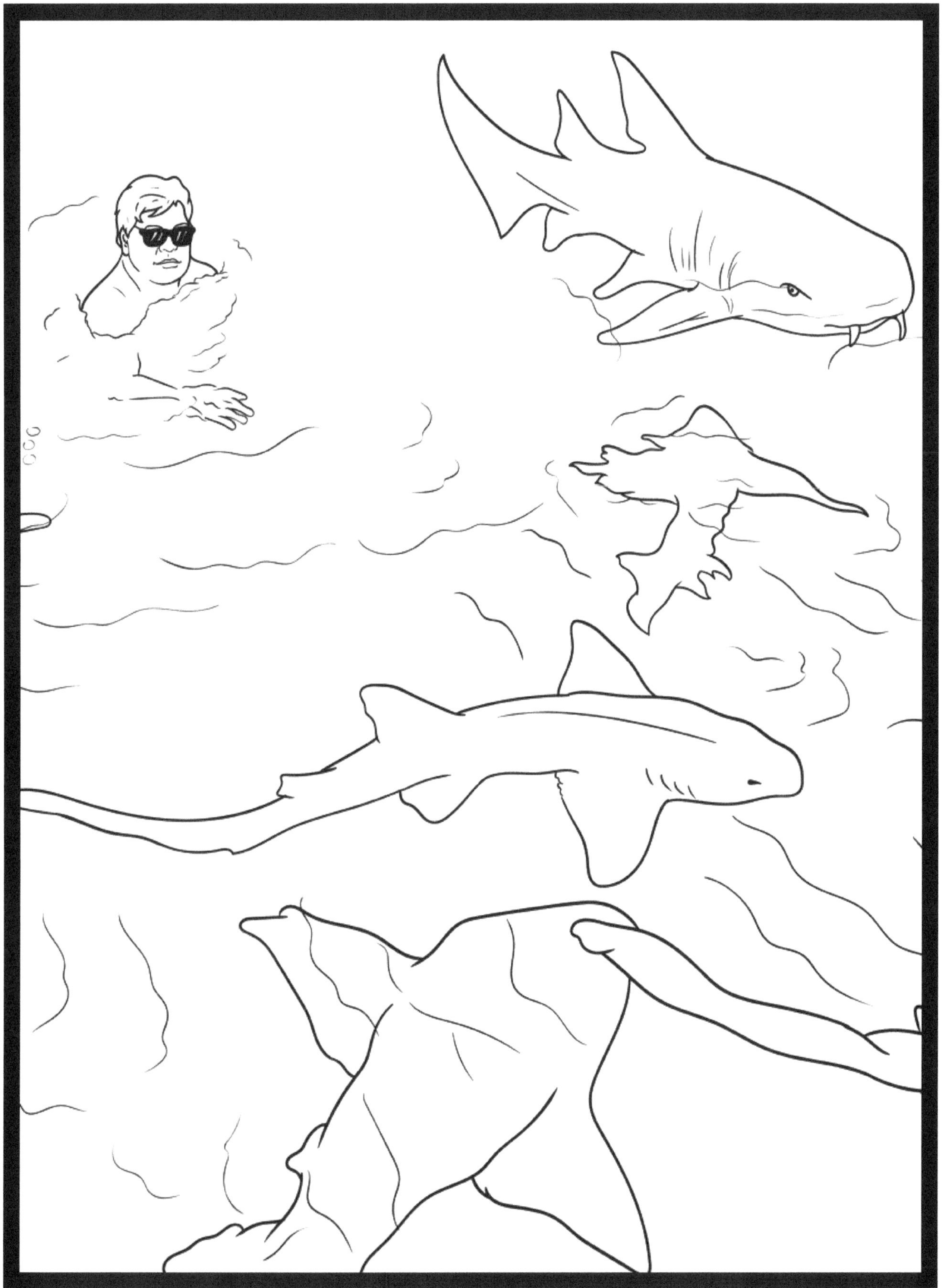

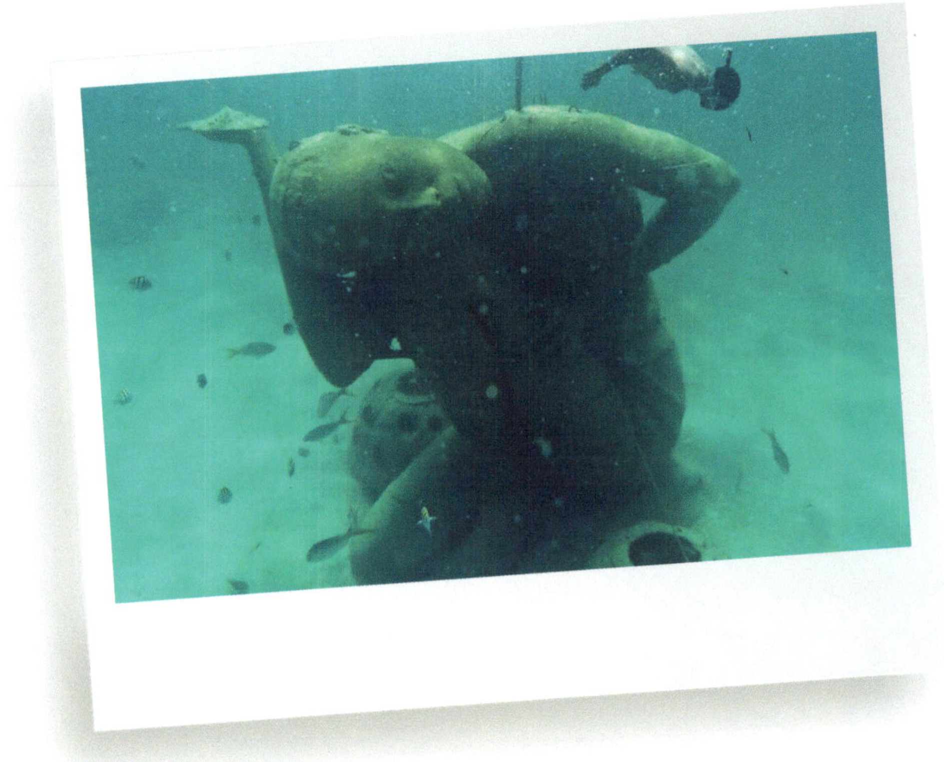

CLIFTON PIER, BAHAMAS

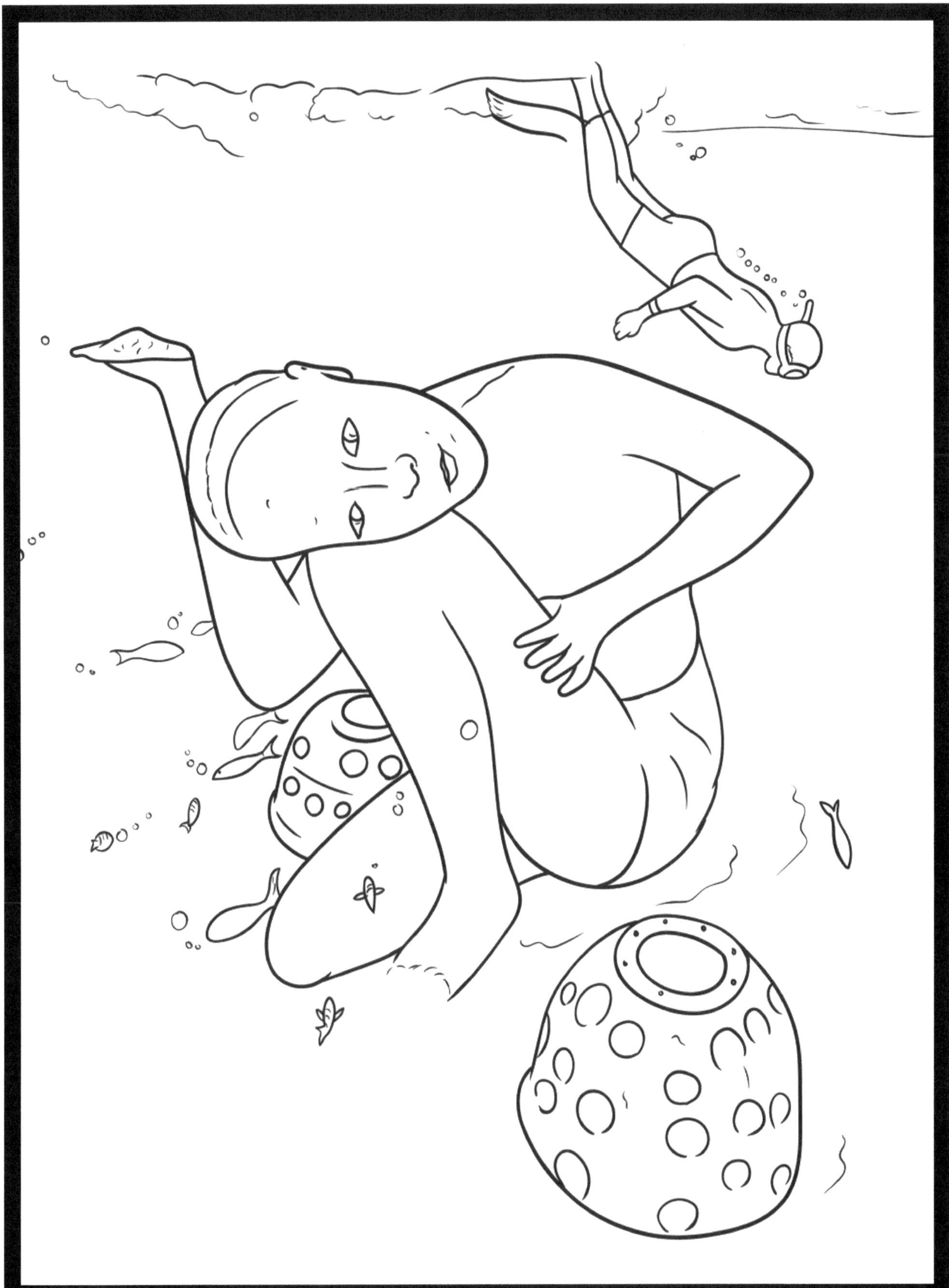

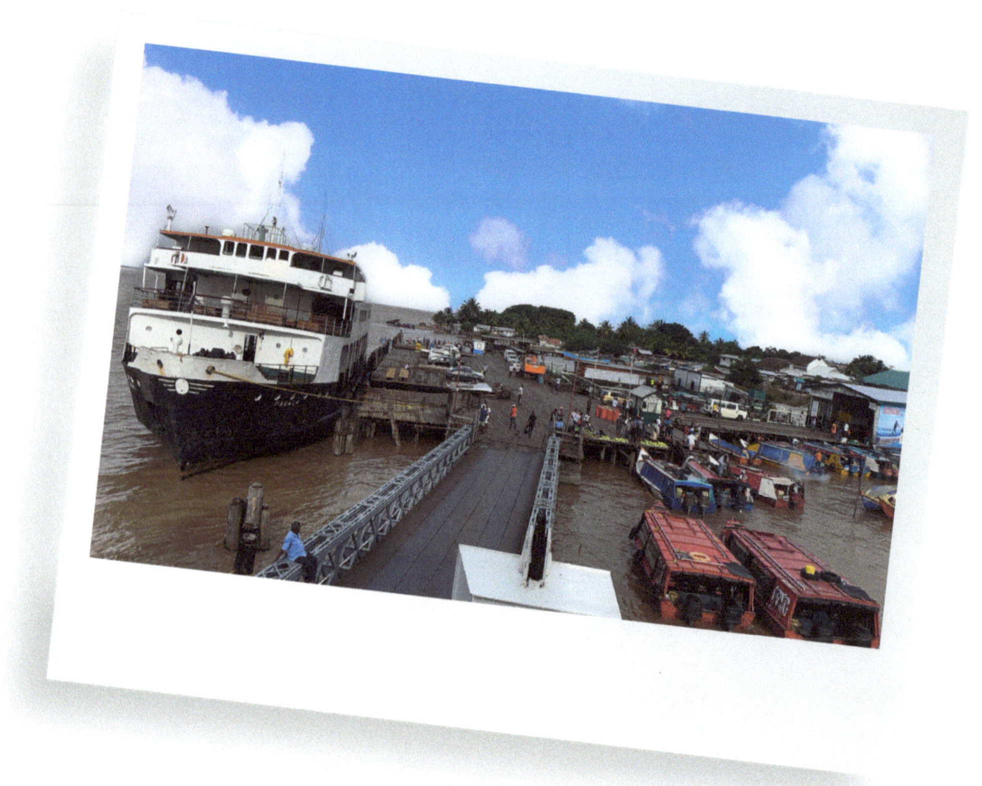

PARIKA, GUYANA

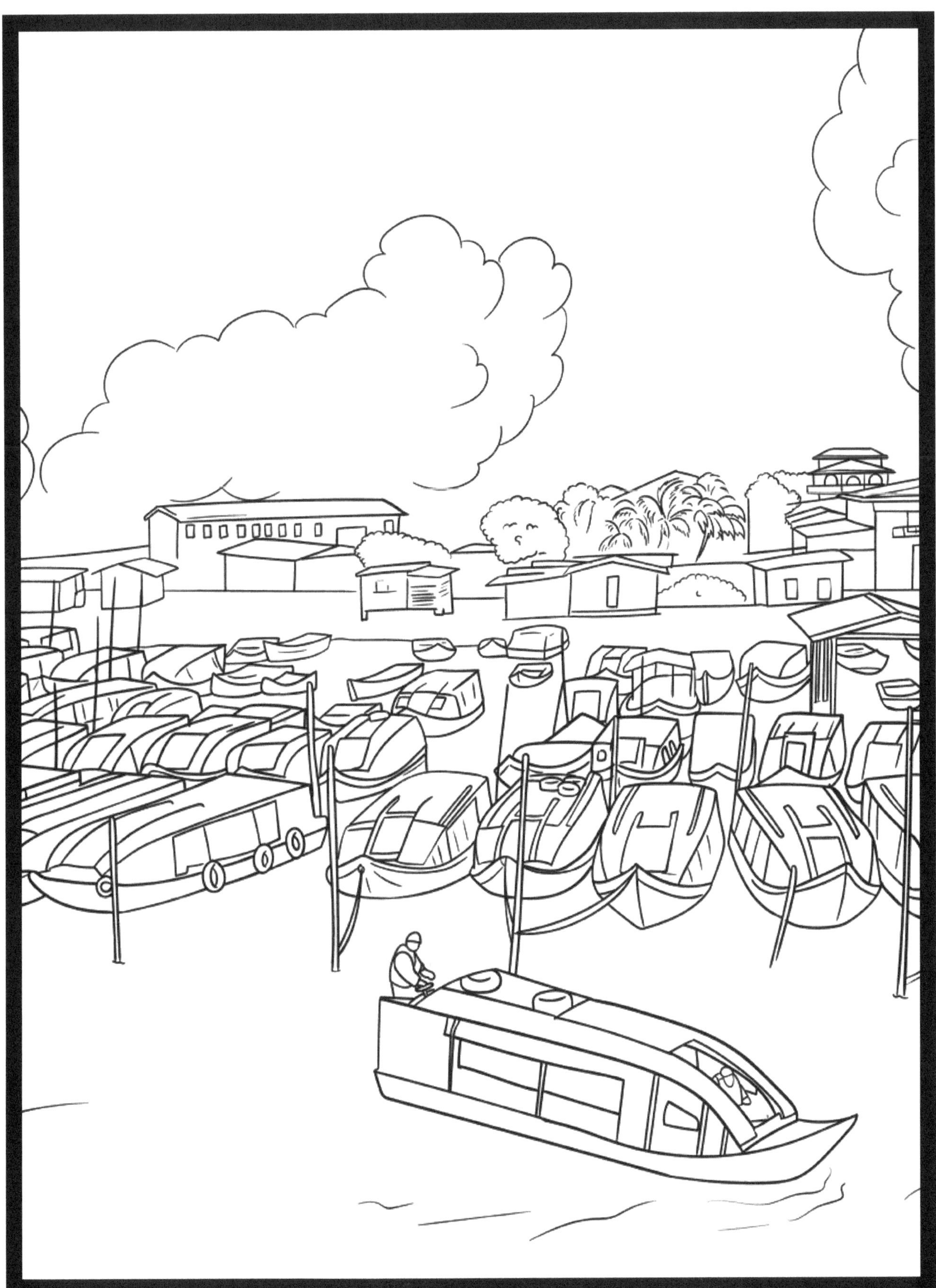

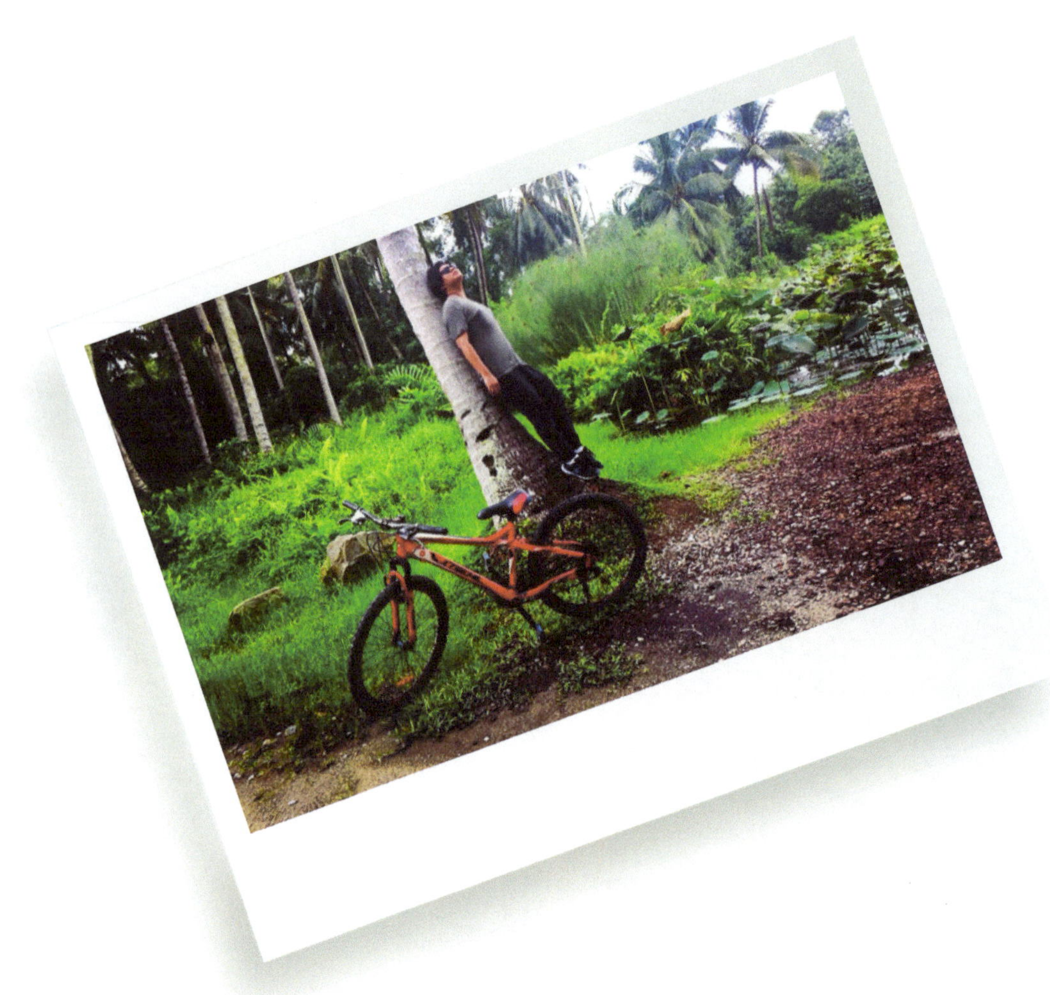

PALAU UBIN, SINGAPORE

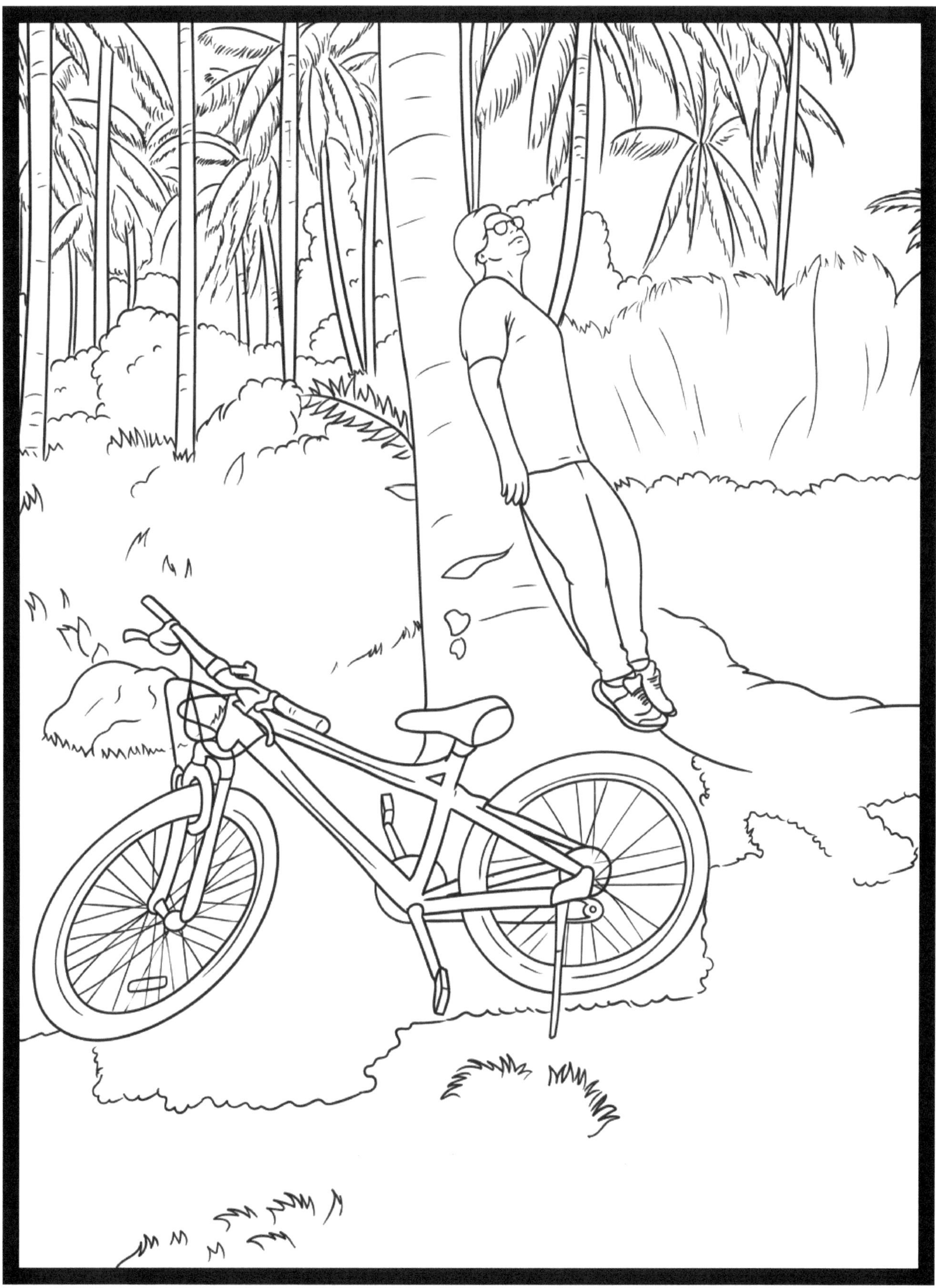

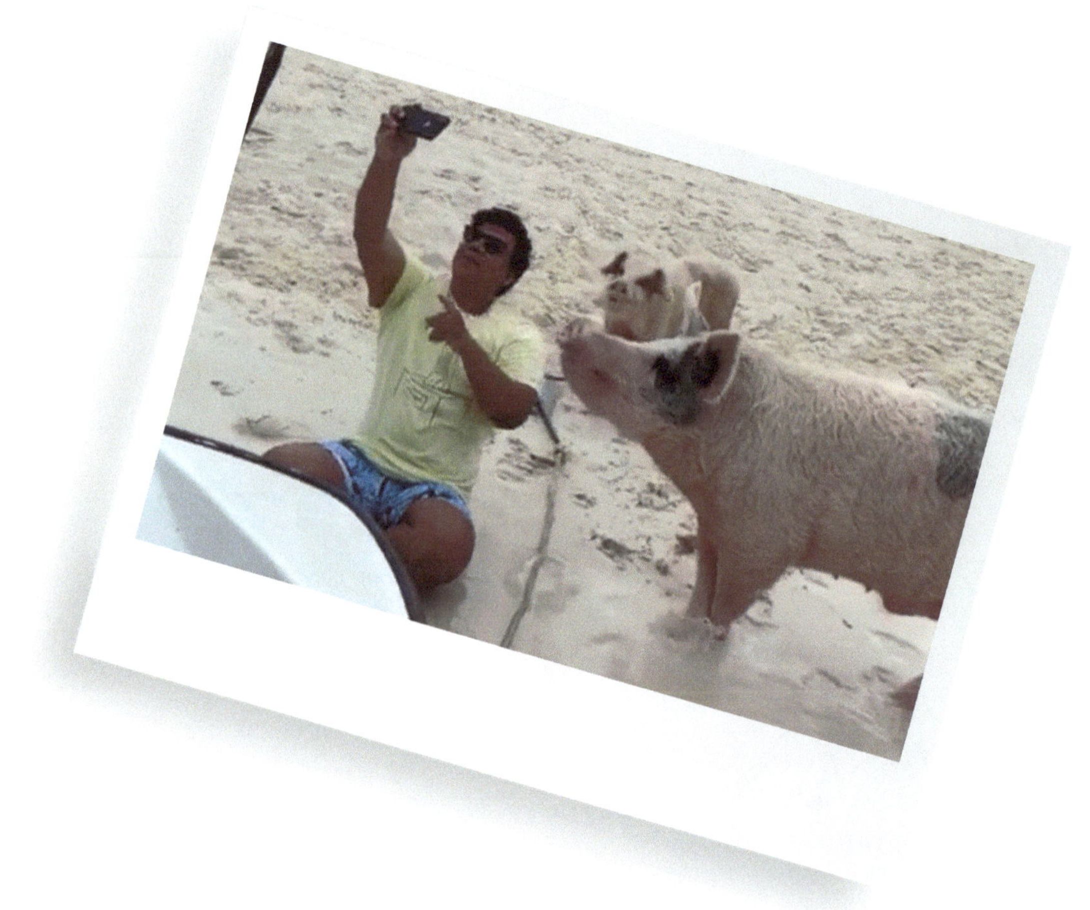

PIG ISLAND, EXUMA

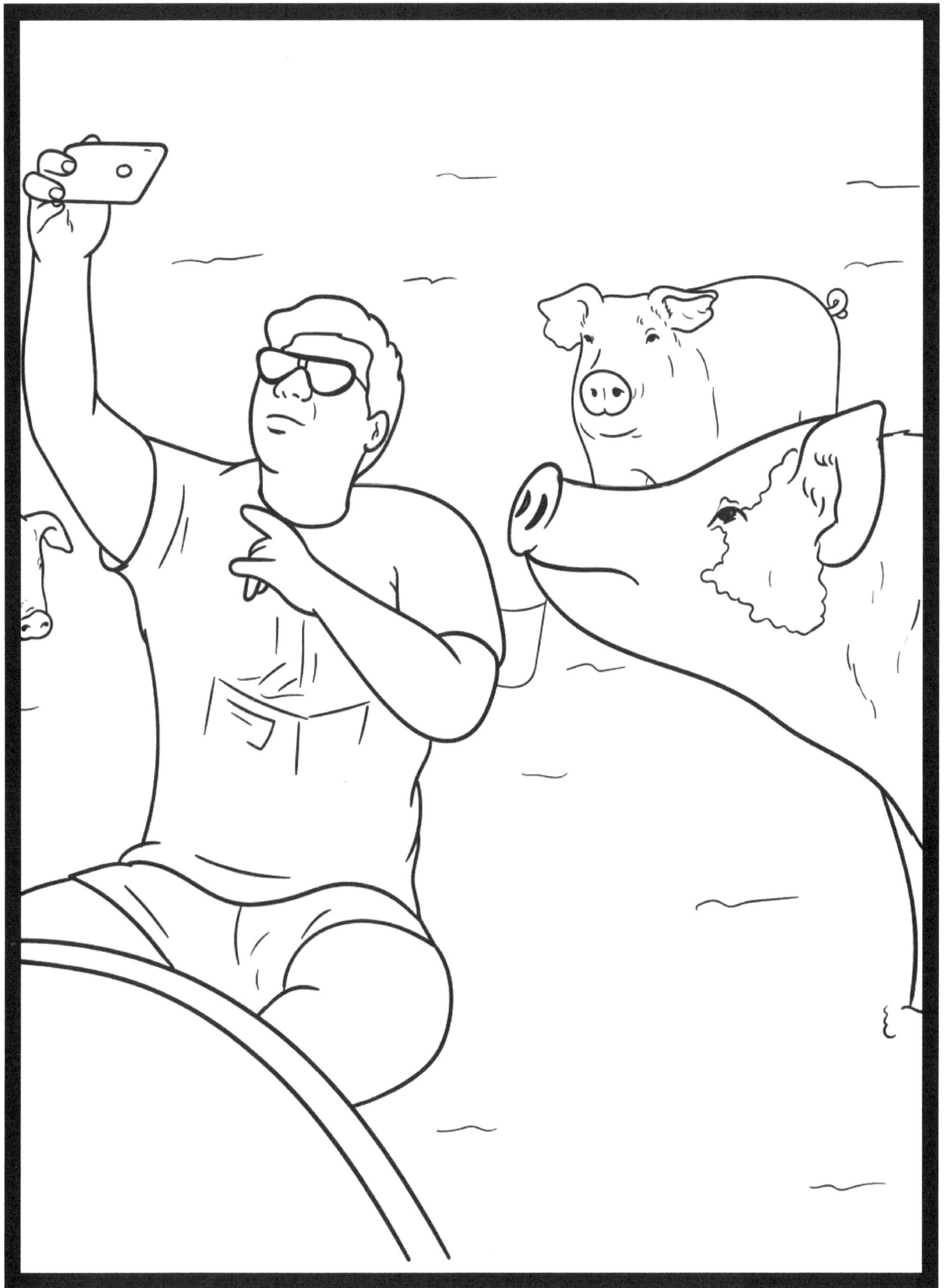

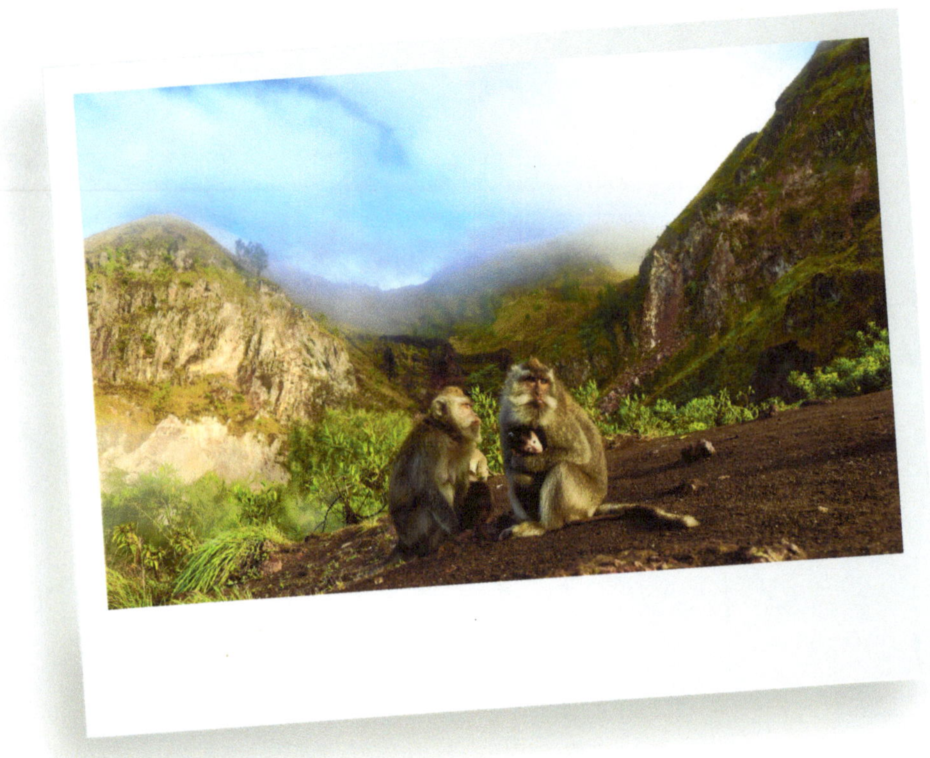

MOUNT BATUR, INDONESIA

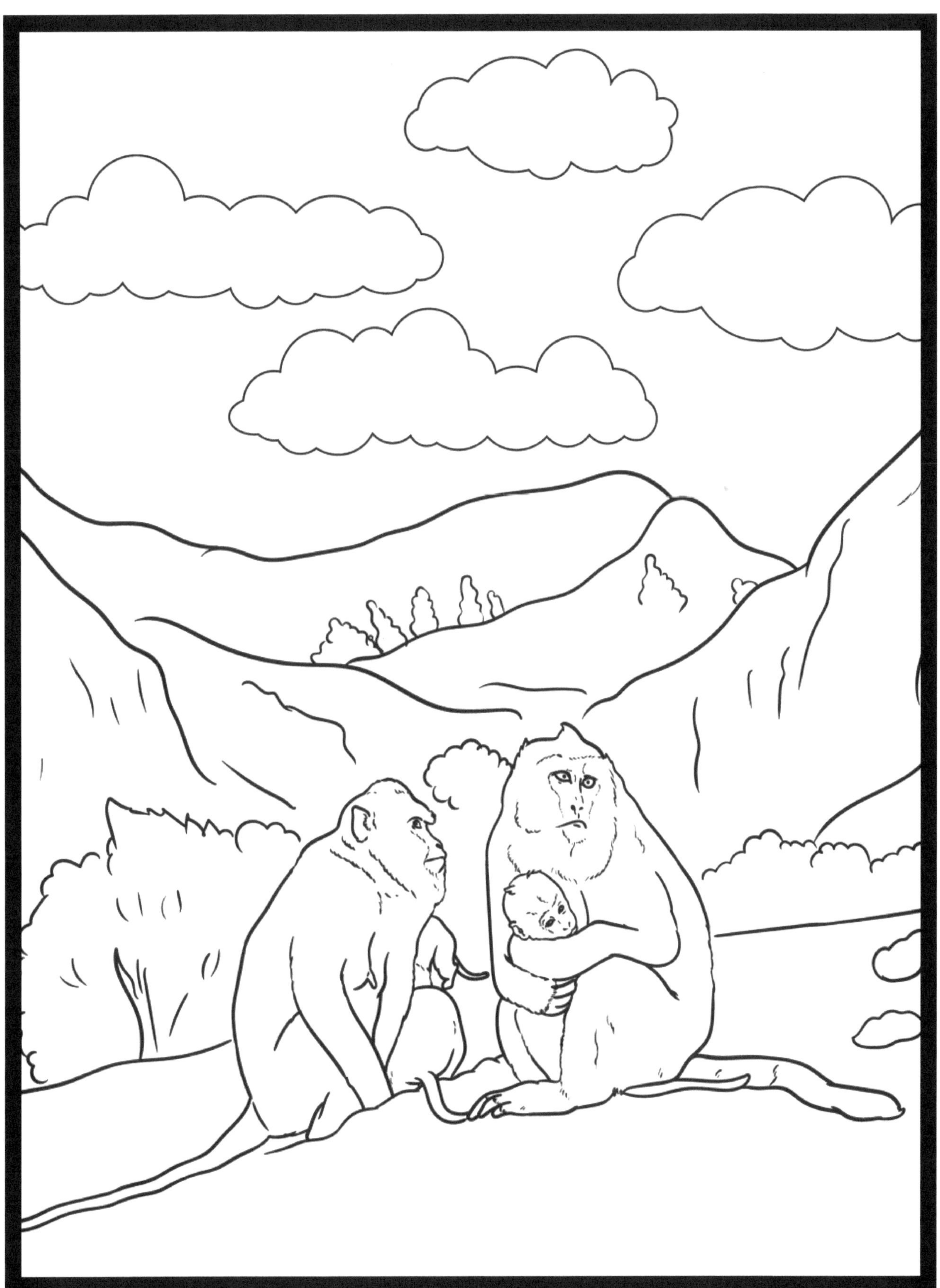

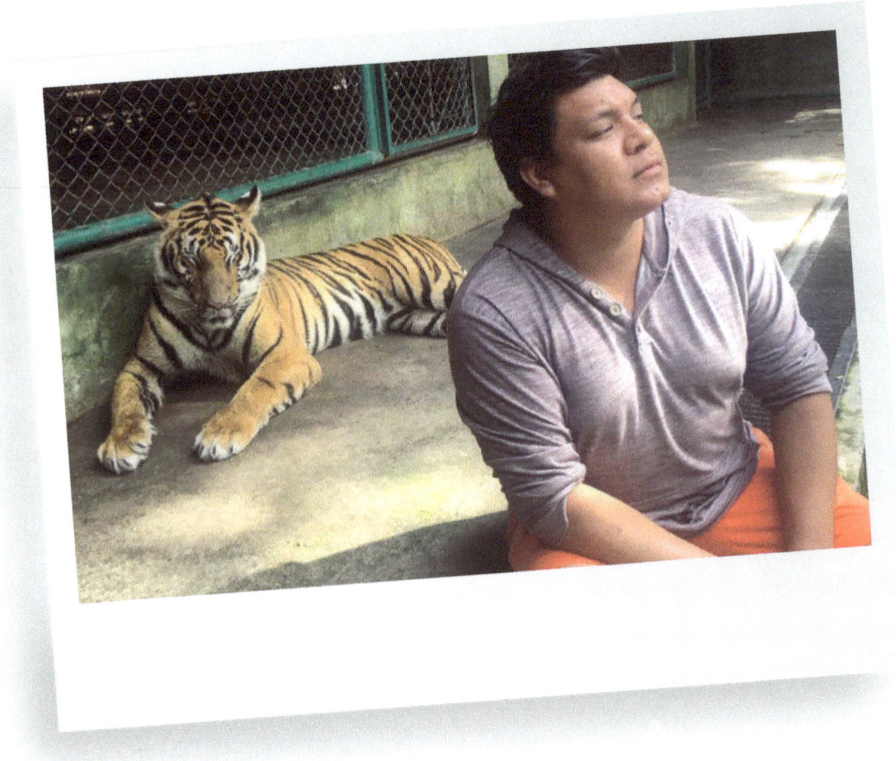

PHUKET, THAILAND

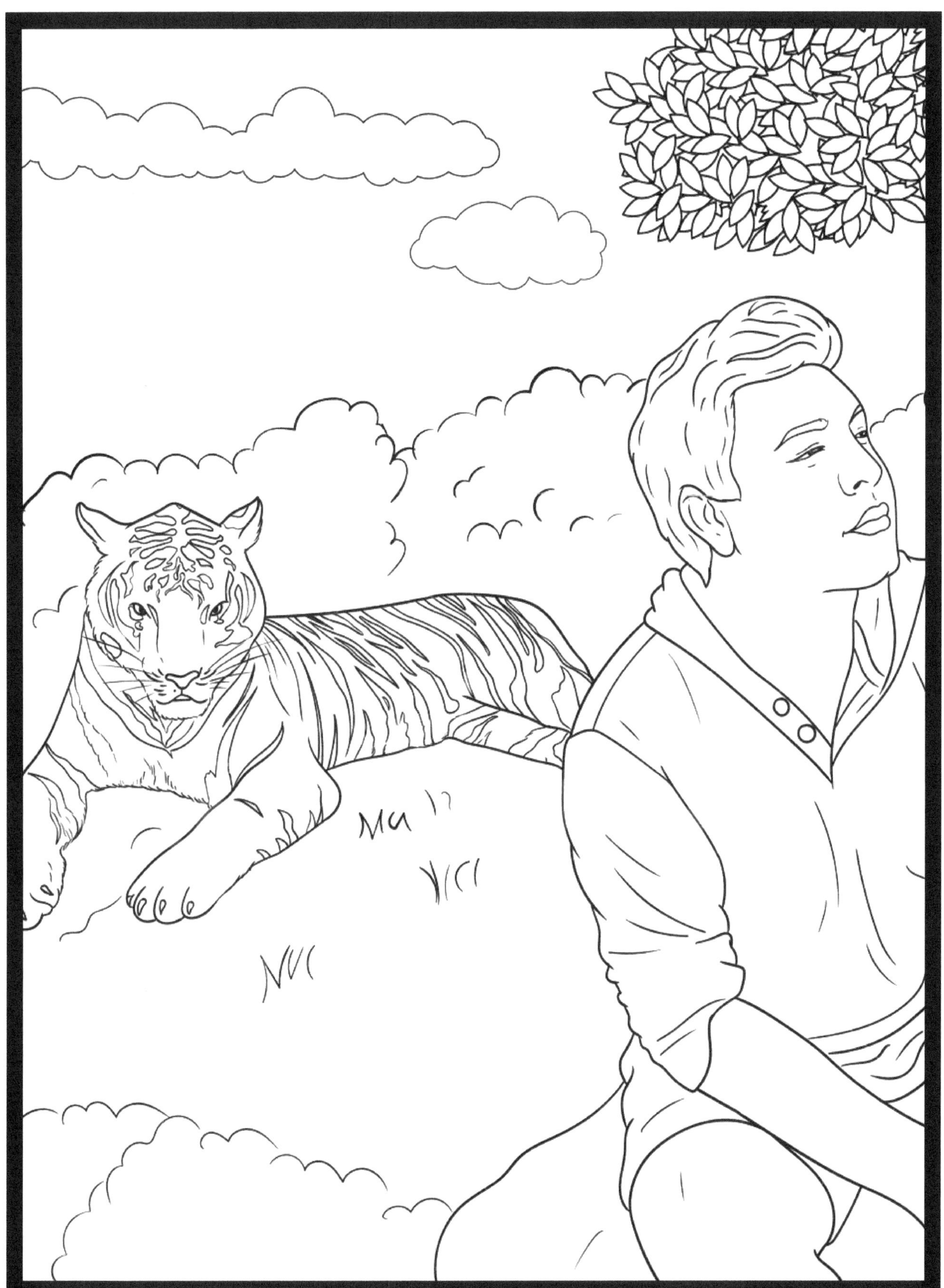

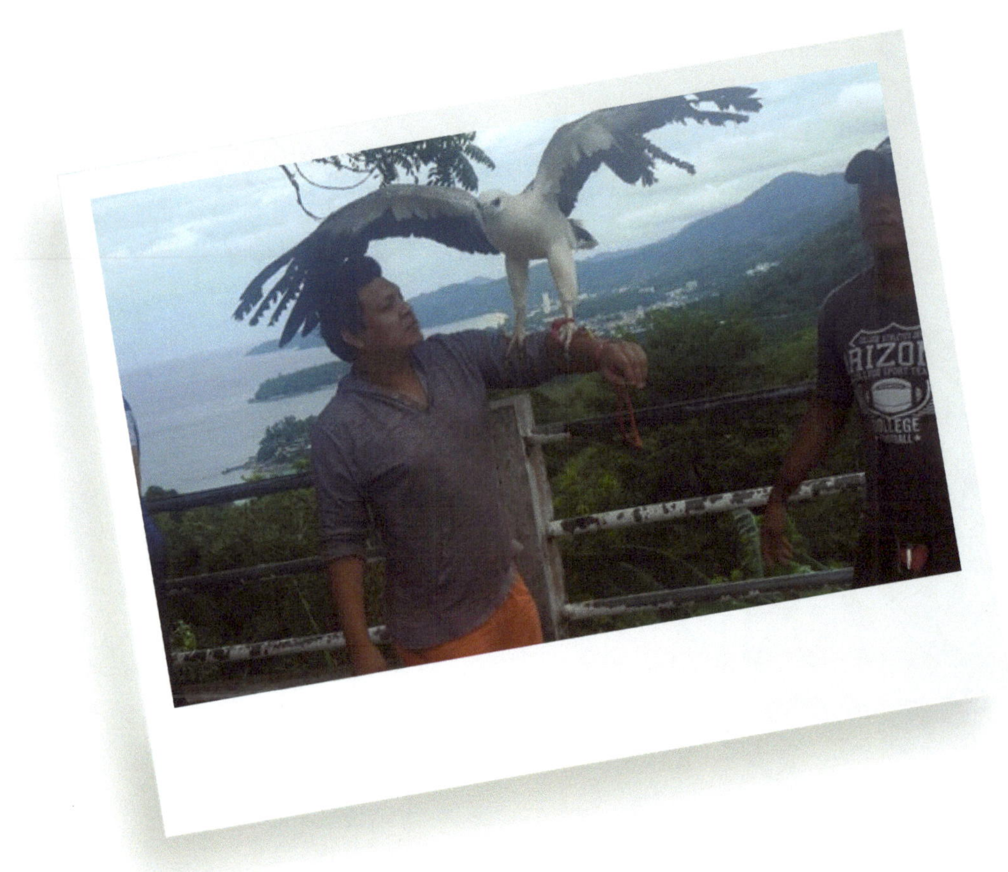

PHUKET, THAILAND

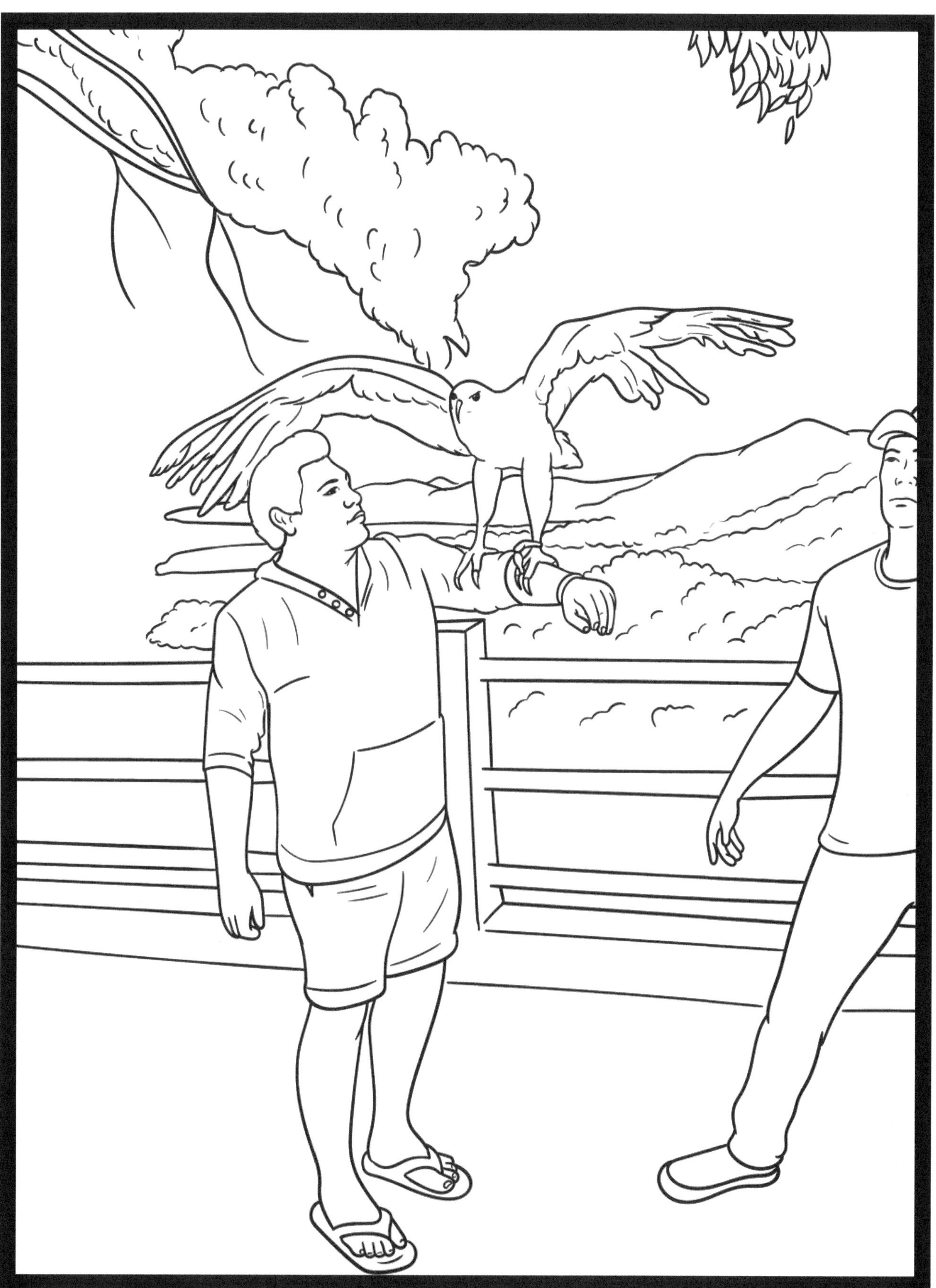

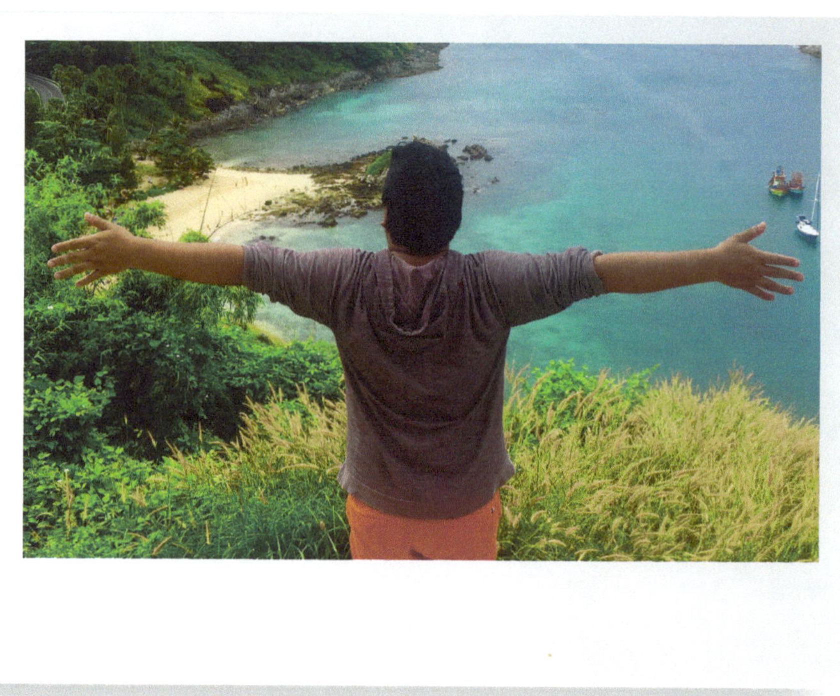

PHUKET, THAILAND

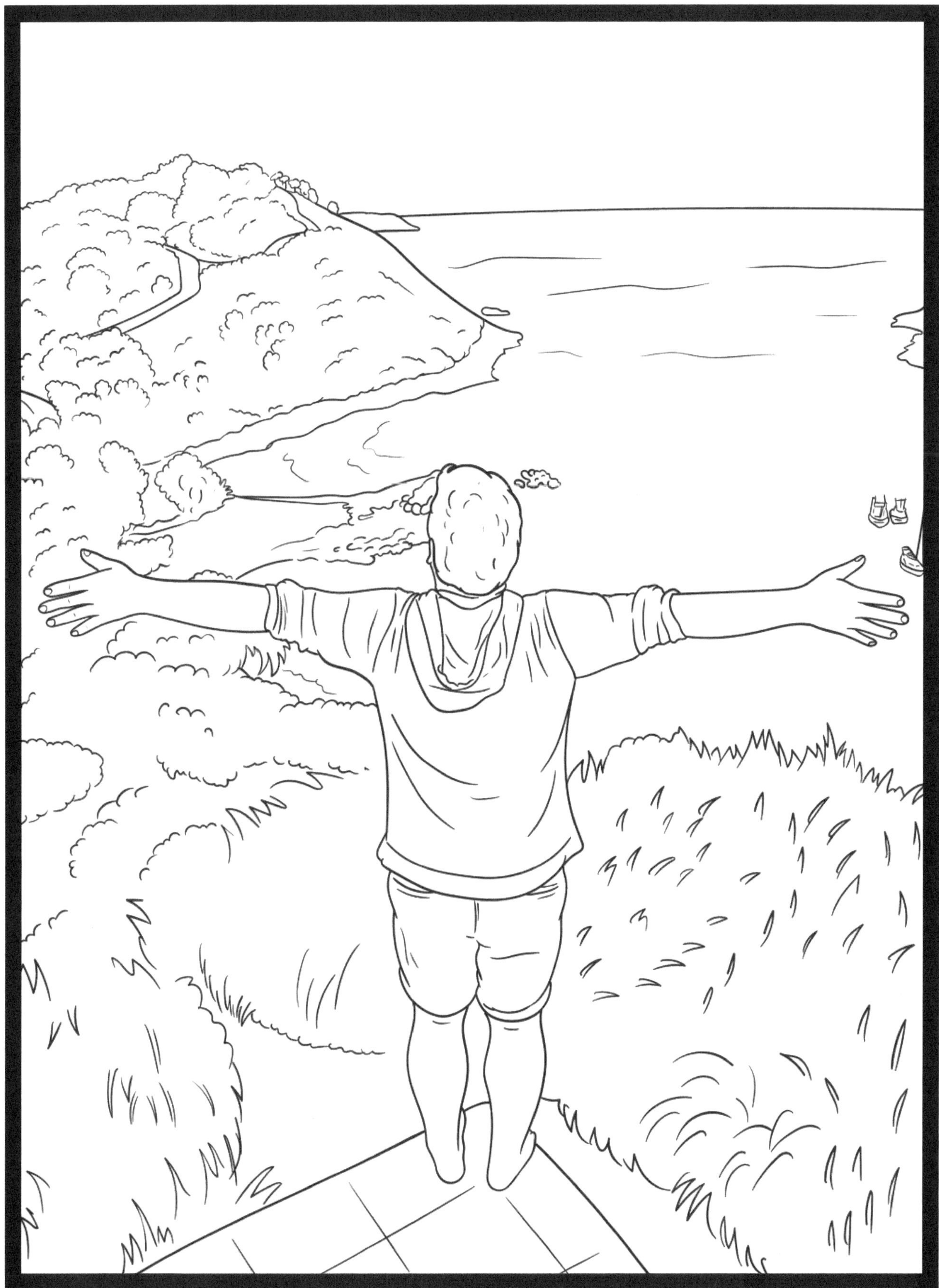

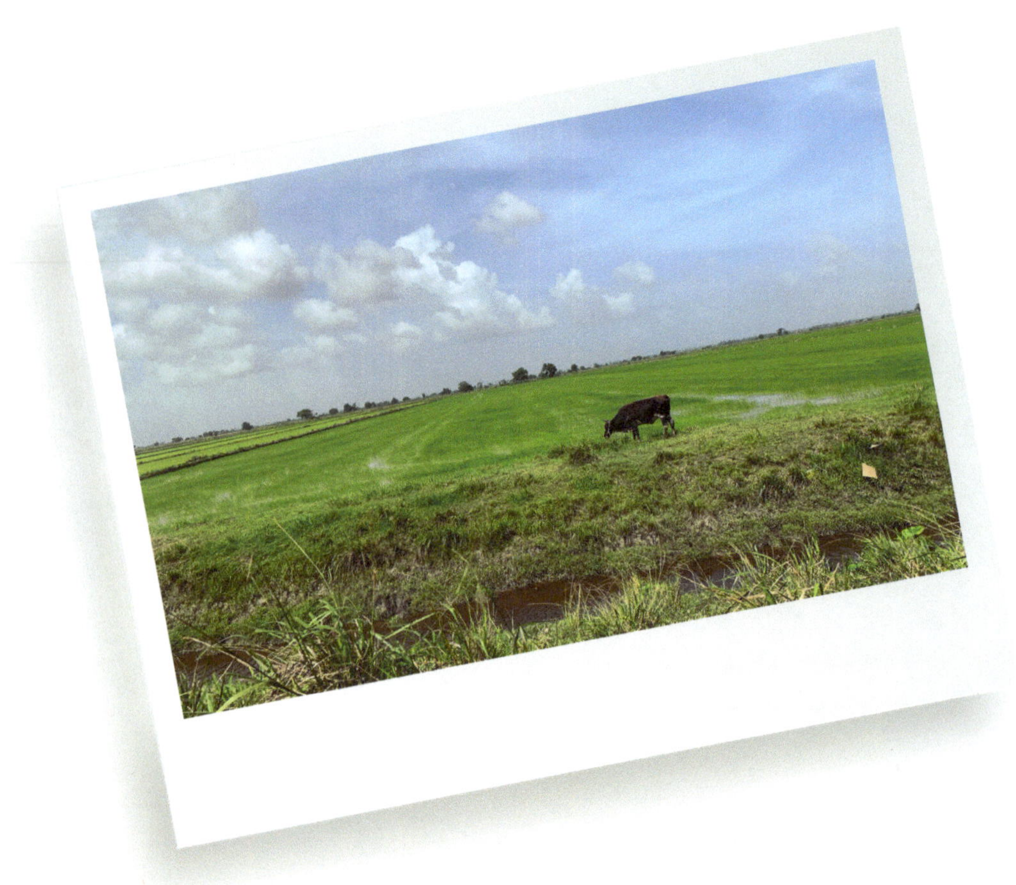

ESSEQUIBO, GUYANA

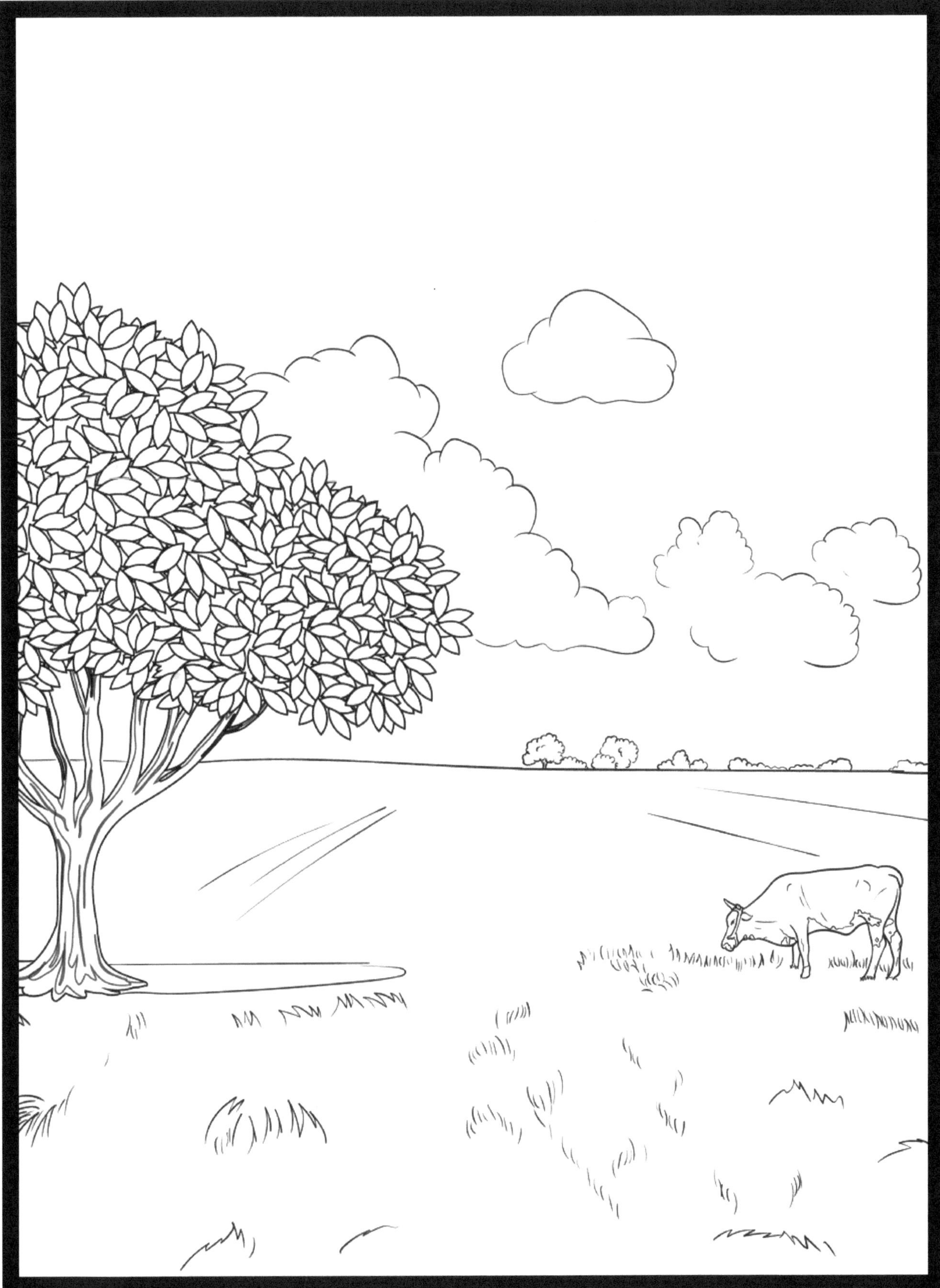

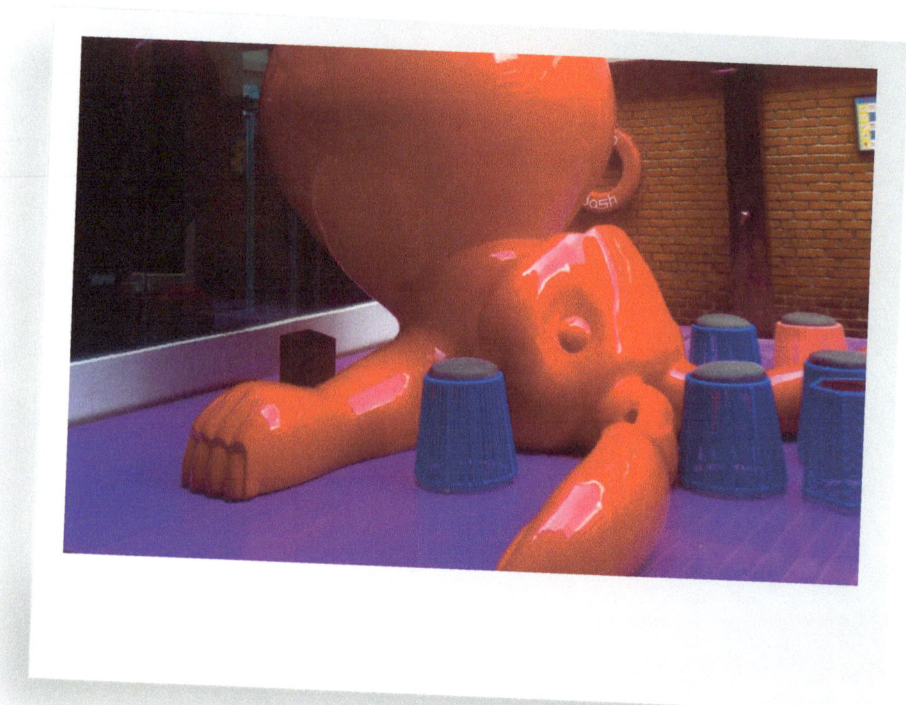

DENPASAR, BALI

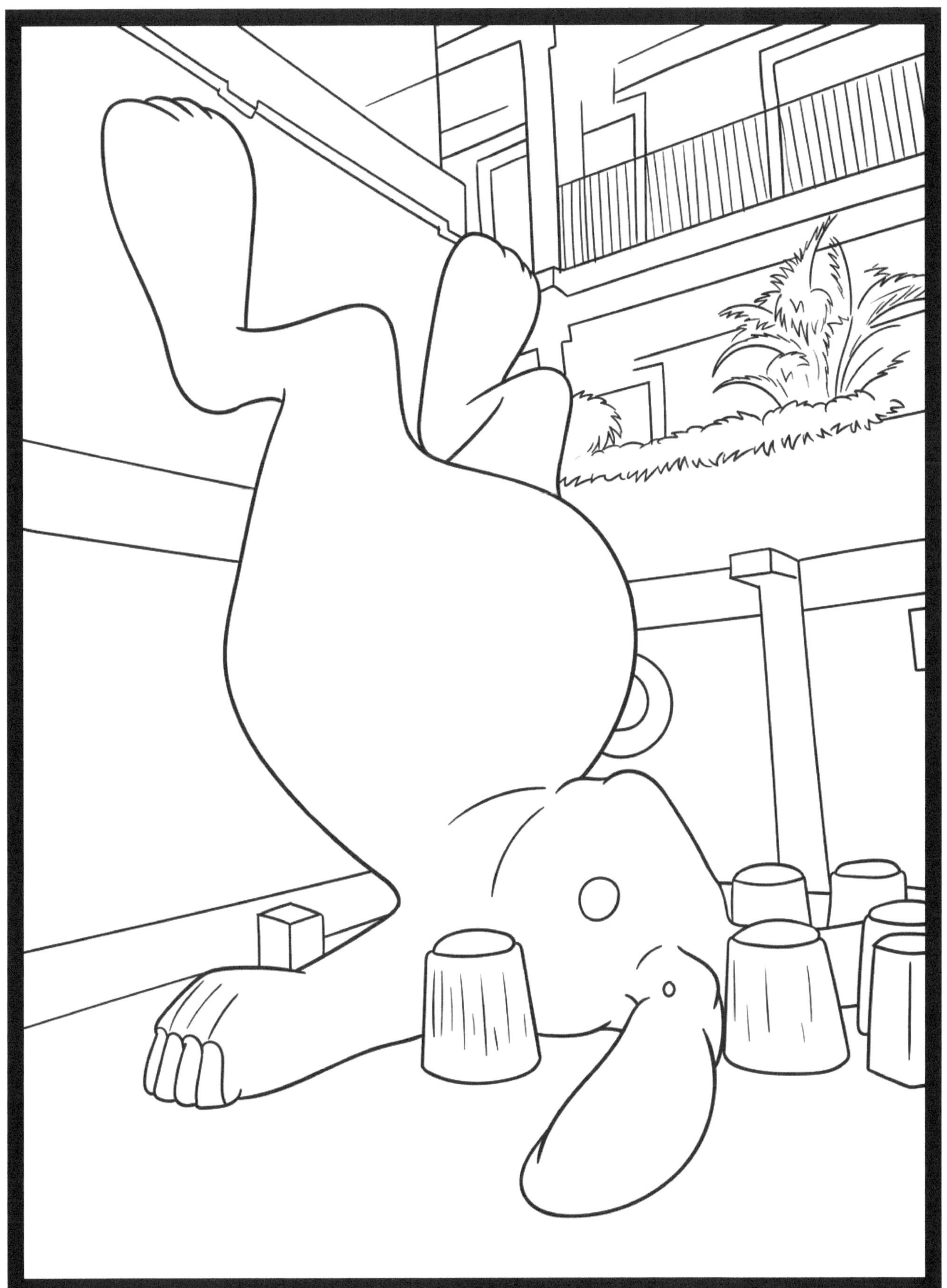

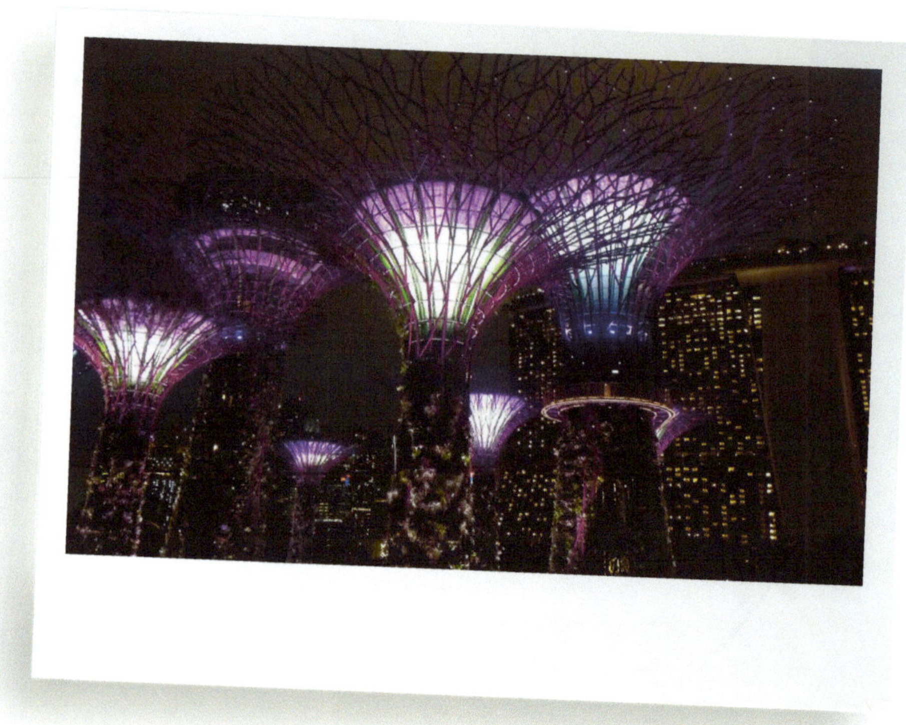

SINGAPORE

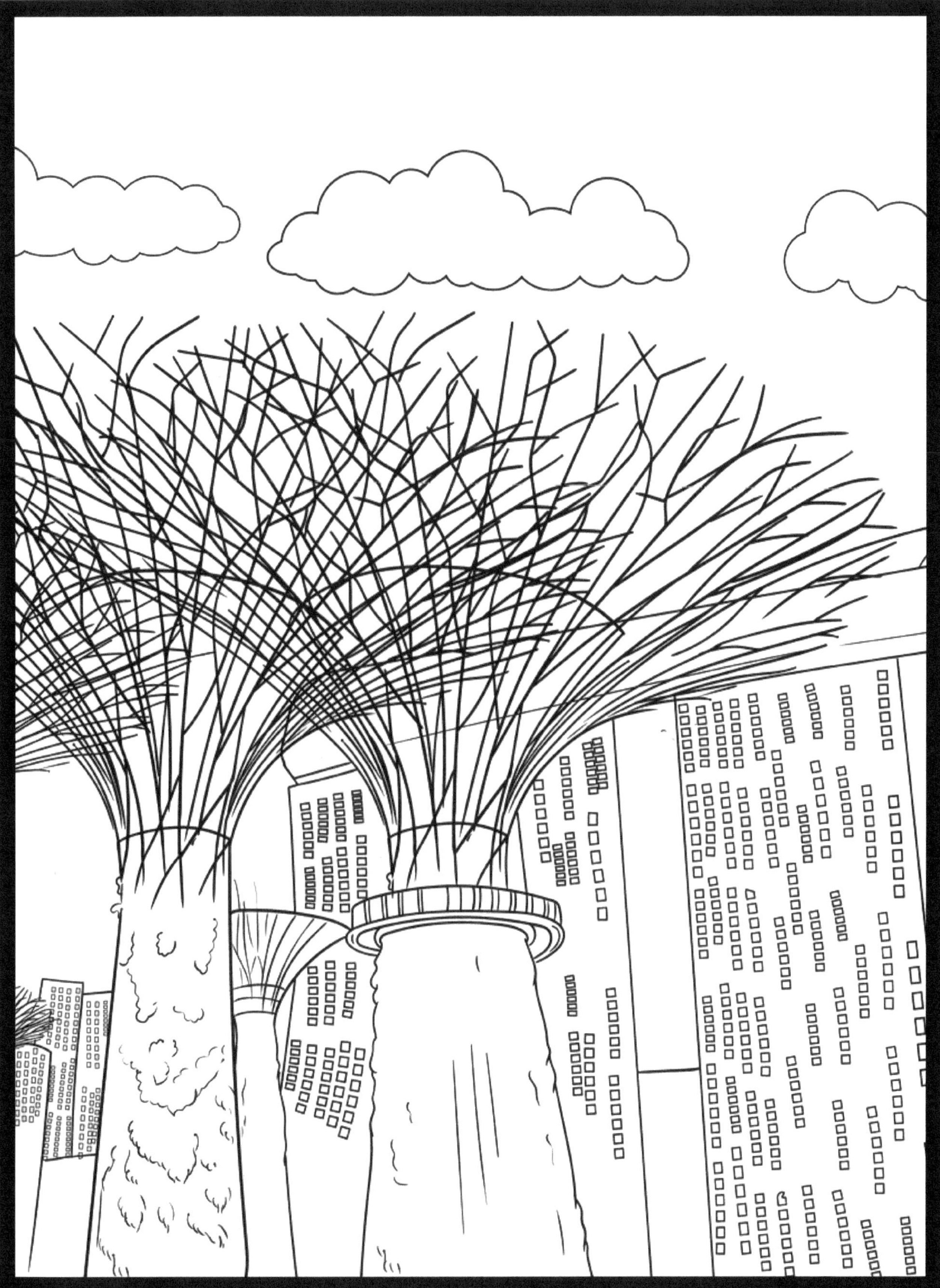

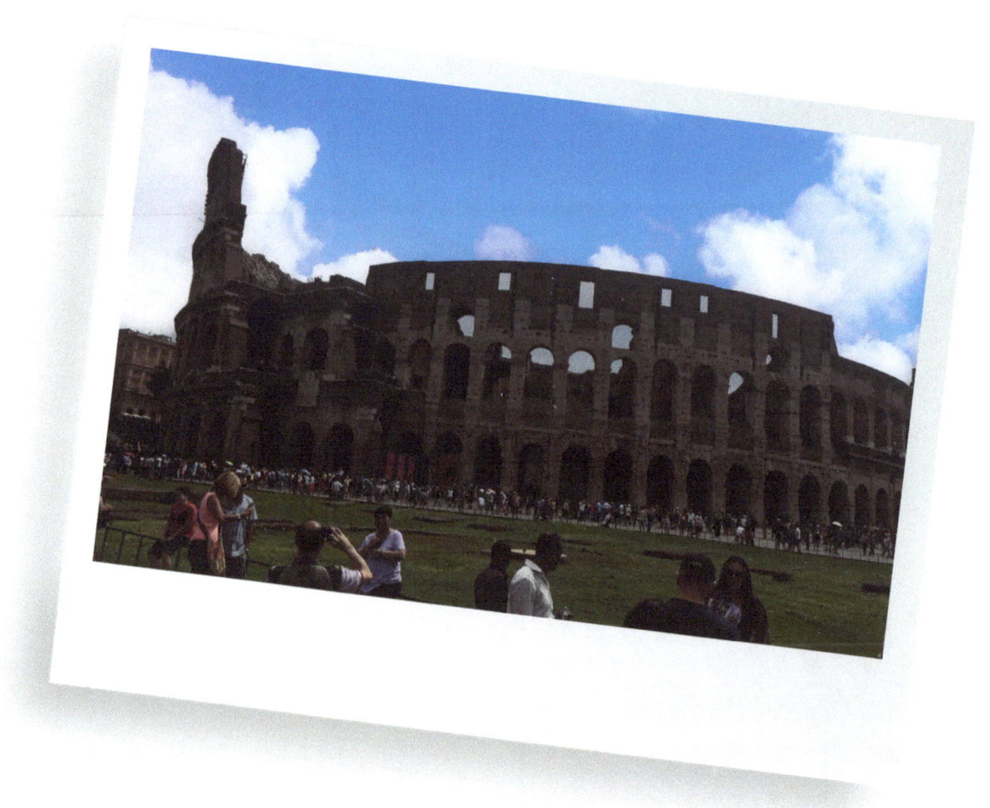

ROME, ITALY

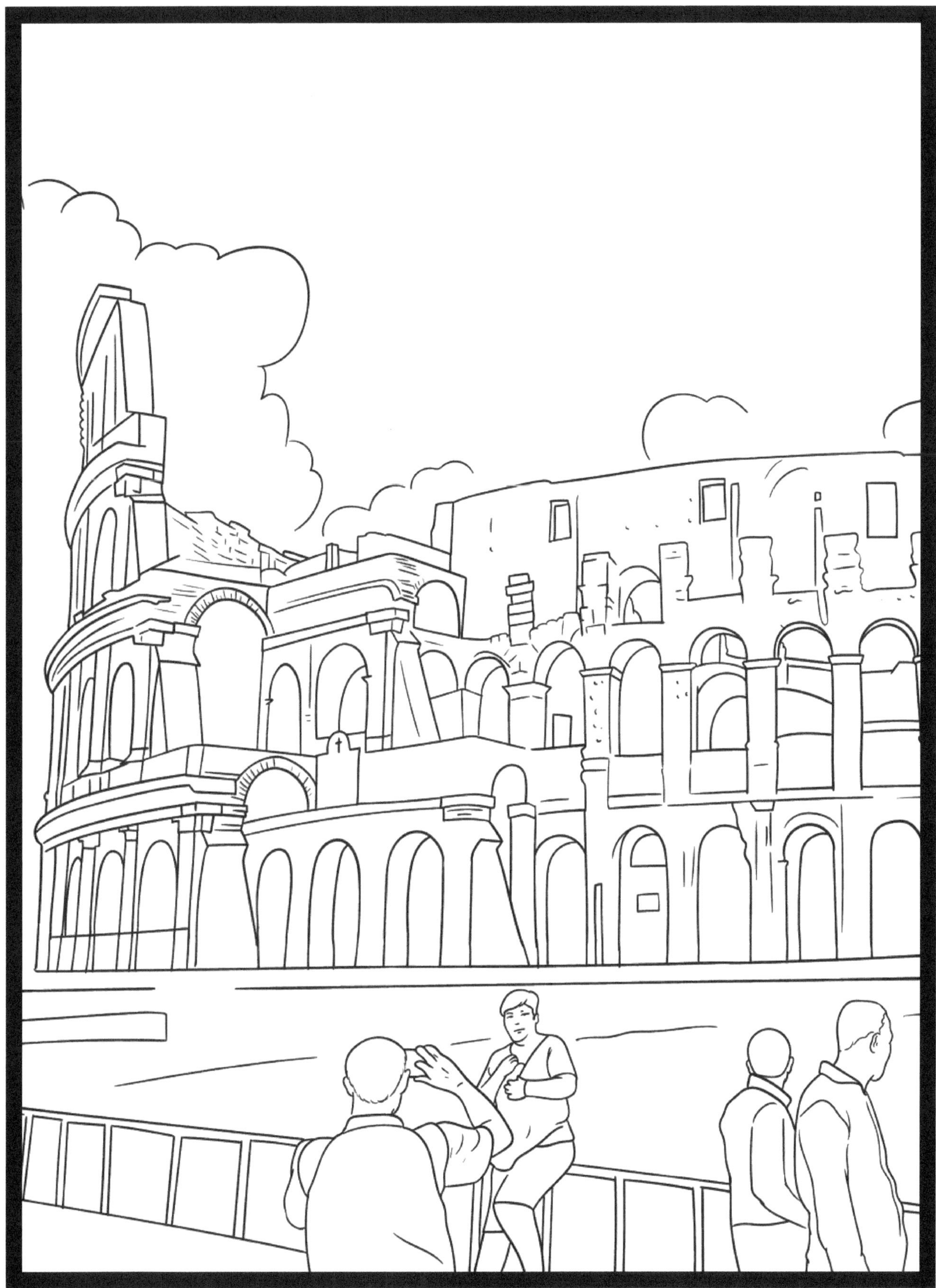

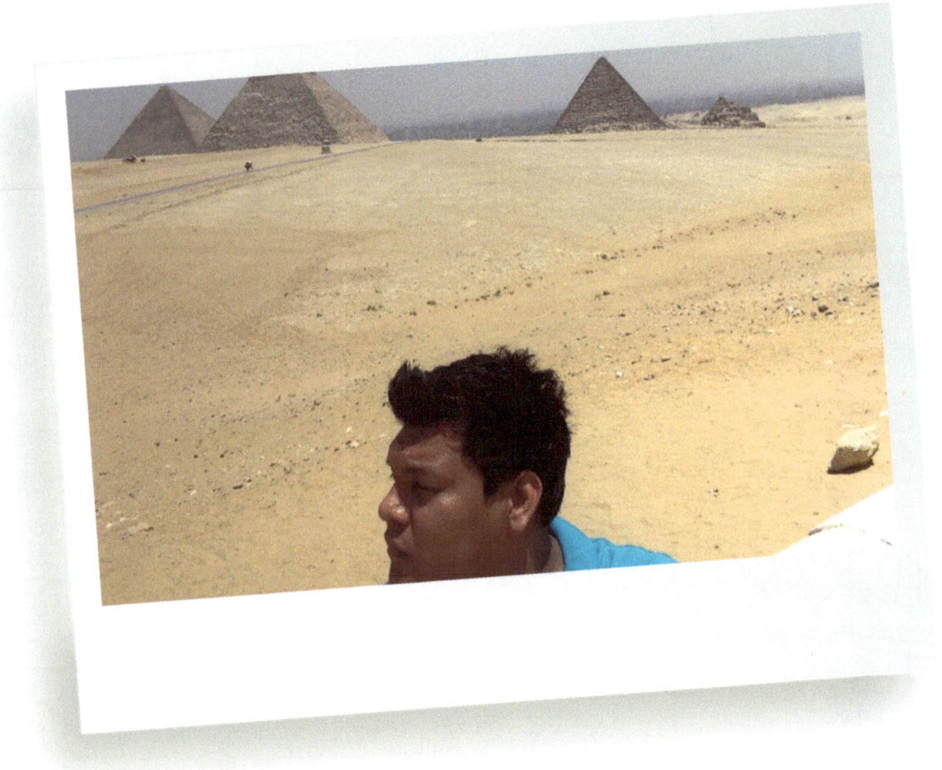

GIZA, EGYPT

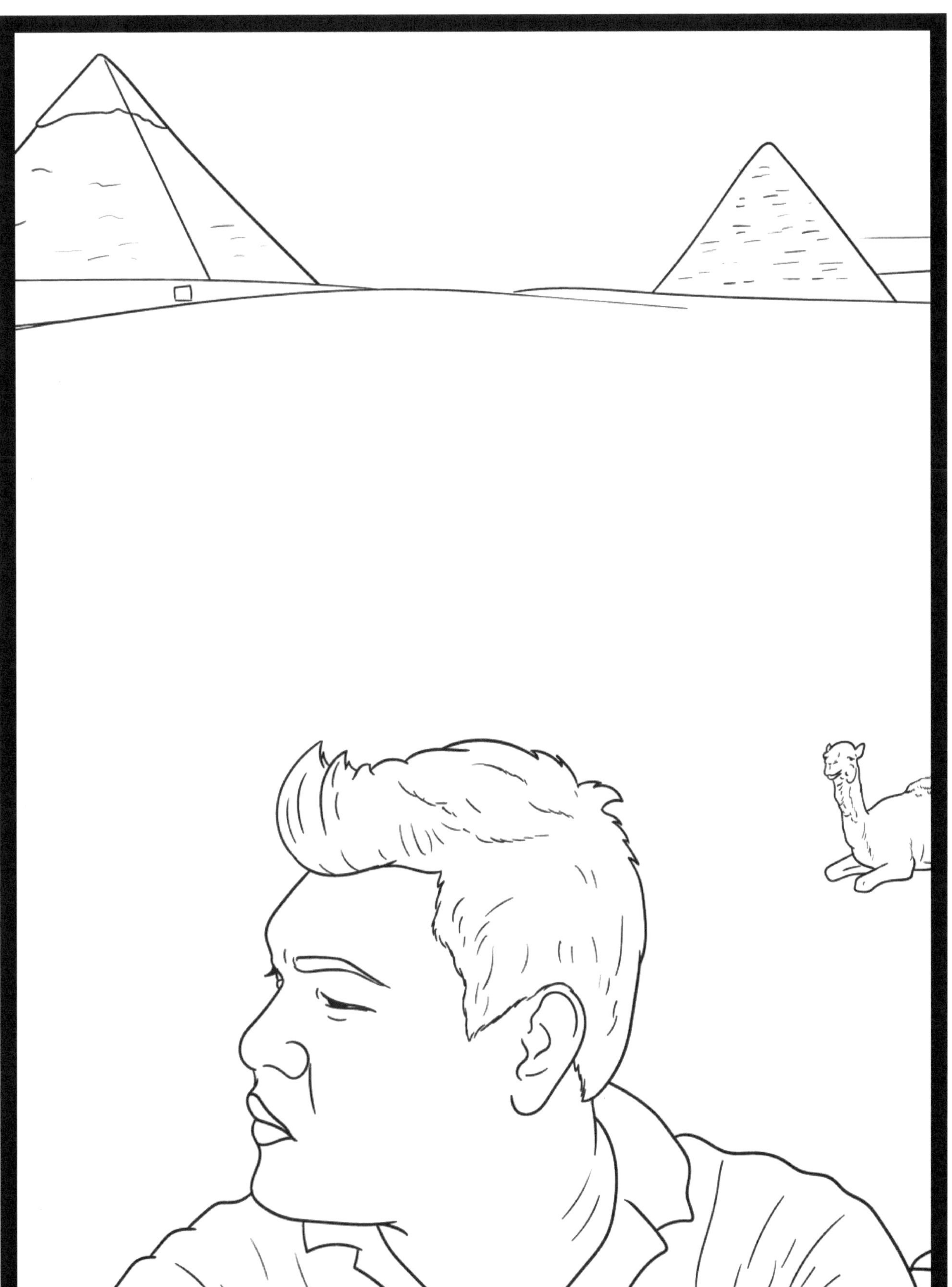